The Alchemy of the Word:
Writers Talk About Writing

Edited by Nicola Morris and Aimee Liu

The Alchemy of the Word:
Writers Talk About Writing

Edited by Nicola Morris and Aimee Liu

ISBN: 978-0-9826556-4-1

Cover design: Stelli Munnis
Book layout: Cherie Poland

Published in the United States by Coimbra Editions,
San Francisco, California

California Institute of Arts and Letters
www.calartsandletters.org

ACKNOWLEDGEMENTS

Rebecca Brown's essay, "Failure, An Appreciation," was reprinted in a different form in *The Stranger* magazine on Feb 9, 2010.

Michael Klein's essay, "Playing by Ear," was published in *Poets & Writers* magazine, May/June 2000. Reprinted by permission of the publisher, Poets & Writers, Inc., 90 Broad Street, Suite 2100, York, NY 10004. www.pw.org

Michael Klein's essay, "Women Who Write the World," was published in *Provincetown Arts*, 2002 and is reprinted by permission of the publisher, Provincetown Arts.

John McManus' essay "Outnumbering the Dead," first appeared in a journal called *Grist: The Journal for Writers* in 2009.

Victoria Nelson's essay, "Reading at the Bottom of the World," was published in *Raritan*, Winter, 2004.

Paul Selig's essay, "Dr. Edie Gives A Commencement Speech," from the play *Mystery School* was previously published in *The Best American Short Plays of 1995–1998*, Applause Books.

Paul Selig's essay, "Commencement Speech," was previously published in the online literary journal *Qarrtisiluni* in June, 2008.

TABLE OF CONTENTS

Preface

To be honest with you, I had no idea what a low residency program was when I first came to teach at Goddard College some seventeen years ago. I understood the basic format—students would gather with faculty on campus for two ten-day sessions, or residencies, each year, and the rest of the time they would work one-on-one with faculty advisors by mail. But as a teacher I wrongly assumed it to be a lightweight venture, a part-time gig to make some money while I went about my real business as a working writer. After all, my own experience as a graduate of a traditional conservatory program had led me to believe that the point of MFA programs was simply to buy students time to write before they jumped into active competition in the literary world. I was in for quite a surprise.

What greeted me at my first Goddard residency was a kind of community I had never dreamed possible; a non-competitive community where students' individual learning needs were put in the forefront of their education. The program was far more academically rigorous than I could have imagined and the faculty—well, they were teachers of the first order, and I found their dedication to shepherding a new generation of writers came from a place of deep generosity, wisdom and integrity.

It is now my great pleasure to introduce you to the faculty of Goddard's MFA in Creative Writing Program in the best way possible— through their own writings about the teaching of writing and living the writer's life. They are an extraordinary bunch; fine writers who are dedicated to the teaching of writing as its own art form, and I believe that you will realize this through your own reading of their work.

I should explain that a Goddard residency is like no other. At the start of each semester, students and faculty travel from all over the world to the Goddard campus—either the one in Plainfield, Vermont, or the one at our second home in Port Townsend, Washington—for a week of workshops, lectures, seminars, talks and readings, many built around a "residency theme." Each residency has a keynote address, and many of the selections in this anthology have been culled from them. Each residency also has a graduation ceremony and speaker, and some of the commencement speeches by faculty have also been included here.

I had the privilege of hearing all of these pieces as they were delivered, and I was thrilled to become a student again as I listened to my colleagues lecture about what matters to them most: writing and the writing life. I am glad that you can join me here now as we revisit them.

Paul Selig, Director
MFA in Creative Writing Program, Goddard College
November 10, 2010

INTRODUCTION

al·che·my

noun \' al-kə-mē\

1: an archaic form of chemistry with philosophical and magical associations, meant to change base metals into gold and tap the secret of eternal life

2: a power or mysterious process of transformation, esp. changing the ordinary into the extraordinary

Words become us. Our lives become our words. Our stories, experiences, thoughts, and dreams are the stuff our words are made of. To this formidable alchemy the essays in this collection speak.

The Alchemy of the Word is no ordinary book about writing, reading, and the writing life. Here you will travel to the wellsprings of literary inspiration. With poet Kenny Fries you'll discover that "Japanese gardens hold within them a microcosm of what it means to be alive in a mortal world... There is nothing more constant than change." You'll join playwright Rogelio Martinez as he maps his storytelling voyage from childhood in Cuba to outer space. And read aloud the words of silence that gave novelist and memoirist Rahna Reiko Rizzoto her voice—"That is the voice of displacement. The sound of exile."

This collection of essays, originally delivered as keynote or commencement addresses to students in Goddard College's Master of Fine Arts program in Creative Writing, speaks to the many thematic undercurrents, sometimes running clear as surface water, sometimes swirling in the depths, that give the processes of writing and reading their transformative power. Susan Kim exposes subtext as the "ghost in the machine" of storytelling. Elena Georgiou writes of the sense of belonging and acceptance that she, a child of an immigrant community in London, gained after discovering the literature of Alice Walker, Toni Morrison, and Audre Lorde. Michael Klein reflects on the currents that impelled him to create the first anthology of poetry about the AIDS crisis: "One of the tasks of a poem was to make something lyrical out of something horrible. Everything felt like I was reading myself back into being a writer."

But the alchemy of the word is also a practical business, a fact that screenwriter Neil Landau laments in "What We Talk About When We Talk About Aesthetic Ambition." Frustratingly, as Rebecca Brown discovers when she charts the "botch" of Herman Melville's *Moby Dick*, it's a business in which success and failure are often indistinguishable and always interwoven. "To fail, then fail better, then fail and fail more, but not to stop." That is the challenge.

This anthology raises as many different points of view as its contributors bring to their diverse styles and subjects. The essays move through the high modernism of Gertrude Stein and Virginia Woolf invoked by Douglas A. Martin, to Ryan Boudinot's meditation on technology's role in "Composing the Wilderness." After musing about "flarf," a recent variation on found poetry, Juliana Spahr wonders whether "All the time that is spent in writing workshops about how to turn a metaphor or where to put that comma is missing some of the more resonant debates about how writing critiques or supports or tears down or holds up or avoids the problematic language practices of our times." Jan Clausen, meanwhile, pushes beyond our times to pose a post-apocalyptic inquiry: "Does a Planet have a Point of View?"

All the contributors to this book are professional novelists, essayists, poets, playwrights, or screenwriters, and all are also members of the faculty of Goddard College's M.F.A. in Writing. Their reflections here prove that, for students and teachers alike, education plays a profound role in the alchemy of the word. Paul Selig, who directs this outstanding graduate program, captures the magic of teaching in the words of his funny, tragic, and incandescent creation Dr. Edie:

> And she began to teach to their potential as if it was the most holy thing ever created. Because in Dr. Edie's mind it was holy. And she saw in each of them the tree that might grow from the seed, and she never once let that vision slip from her mind. And every day, her innocence was reborn. Every day she saw the potential in them, the beauty that was created in them come forth, she was reminded of her own.

As Kyle Bass writes, "I'm showing too much of my hand here." It has been our privilege to compile this collection, but the only way you can appreciate its true value is to read the essays for yourself.

Nicola Morris and Aimee Liu

The Alchemy of the Word:
Writers Talk About Writing

Edited by Nicola Morris and Aimee Liu

I. The Spirit of the Thing

WRITING THE SILENCE

By Rhana Reiko Rizzuto

It was silence that gave me my voice as a writer. It was diaspora. Dispersing. Displacement. Exile.

Everyone's family has diaspora in its history—I thought I would begin by telling you a little about the displacement in my family. In May 1942, several weeks after my mother was born in Los Angeles, she and her entire family—four citizens plus two immigrants who had wanted to become American citizens but were not allowed to because of a law that specifically prevented the Japanese from doing so—were sent to internment camps because the nation they lived in, and belonged to, was at war with the nation where their "blood" originated. Some 120,000 people were sent to camps. They were surrounded by barbed wire, and men with machine guns in watch towers. They lived in military-style barracks, hastily erected, closely divided; entire families were housed in a single small room with dirt floors and only the furniture they could make. They lived with communal bathrooms, with open sewers, eating rationed food in shifts in the mess hall. They had brought only what they could carry; they had lost everything they could not sell; they made a couple of dollars a week working in the camps, which was not enough to pay back taxes on the properties they owned, and so they no longer had homes to return to when they were given a one-way train ticket and $25 at the end of the war and told to leave.

You would think this "displacement" would be worth a family story or two. But we never talked about it. My mother doesn't speak Japanese; she claims not to remember the camps, or to have even heard about them until she was in high school. I heard about the internment only because, when it was finally acknowledged as something that shouldn't have happened, my mother got a small amount of money, and got interested in the place where she began her life. In 1992, she and I went together to Amache—the camp where the family was held—with my grandmother, some of my post-war aunts and about one hundred to one hundred and fifty other people, on buses, with bentos... to discover our history, and there was nothing left.

There was a small graveyard with a few stone markers and some wooden crosses. There was a monument, which had been erected recently and had already been defaced. And there were trees—now fully grown—which had been planted by some of the people around me on the bus. After the ceremony, my mother and I wandered through the prairie grass and the tumbleweeds and found some cracked, overgrown concrete foundations left over from the military-style barracks that were used to house the internees. We paced them off, noting where the potbellied stoves had been, and the walls, and marveling that rooms so small could hold entire families. At lunch, a man in his fifties walked through the community center full of former internees eating home lunches of sushi rice and teriyaki with a yearbook in his hand, searching for anyone in the room who was three when he was three in camp, who might have been in a nearby block, who might have been his friend. My mother might have been, but she didn't remember. My grandmother, furiously smoking cigarettes with her arms crossed in front of her, didn't say.

And never said, actually. My grandmother never said a single thing to me about the camps.

It was obvious to me that there was a story here, which needed to be told but that no one was telling. Shortly after I came back from Amache, I decided to break the silence. I began asking people to tell me about their experiences, and they said the strangest things. They said: "My mom thought it was great because she didn't have to do the cooking." My great uncle told me that the war was "the best thing that had ever happened to the Japanese Americans"—let me review: my family was uprooted, they lost everything, some say my grandfather went a little mad, one of my uncles died fighting for the US government, and the US government wouldn't let his interned parents out of camp to have a funeral. When I couldn't figure out how it could possibly have been a good thing, let alone the best thing, he explained that, before the war, the Japanese Americans were ghettoized, they were not allowed to own land, to become citizens, that they were treated terribly on the West Coast, and that the internment spread them throughout the country, to places where they could begin again, and gave them a way to prove that they were good citizens—Americans, not Japanese.

That is the voice of displacement. The sound of exile.

At the time, this idea had not yet come to me fully. When I was writing that book, and interviewing people, I focused primarily on the silences. The story I was chasing was, in a way, the fact of the silence, the great gap in my family's history, the gap in the nation's history—it seemed incredible that, in the category of things we do not talk about at the dinner table, the wartime experience of hundreds of thousands of people could fit so neatly.

I didn't understand this silence. I decided that it sprung from wanting to fit in. Of not wanting to be labeled as "other" (as traitor, as Japanese, as inferior). The internees were rounded up on the sole basis that they could not be trusted, and they wanted to prove that they were good Americans. That trust was a given, and so could not even be mentioned.

There was also, of course, the nagging feeling that these things do not merely happen—they are not *supposed* to happen in a world of fairness—and so that somehow this must have been "deserved." Silence was a clean up, a fresh start, which everyone has the right to.

Then, several years after that book was published, I got a grant to live in Japan for six months. I went to Hiroshima to interview the survivors of the atomic bombing, and there I encountered another, oddly similar, silence. And I discovered that the narrative of diaspora that I was familiar with was also the narrative of trauma.

If you are speaking to a hibakusha in Hiroshima, in June of 2001, the first thing you will be told is where the person was that August morning. The narrative starts with the blue sky, the heat, the fact that the day was, for some fortuitous reason, different than the others, or maybe not. People will tell you whether they saw the plane and the white speck falling, where they were thrown, when they came to, how they escaped, where they found their families, or found out that they had lost them. They will describe the people walking, the bodies clogging the rivers, the smell of the endless cremations, the swarm of the flies and the maggots in human bodies—all very matter-of-factly, all very rehearsed, because they have been reciting these stories on request for some fifty-five years. The stories will then move on to the moment when it was clear that everyone who was going to die had done so, sprinkled with a few funny episodes about the army rations without a label that someone in the family brought home, cherished until it was revealed to hold only charred remains, or an incomprehensible pool of never before seen food: mayonnaise. There will be, at the end of your interview, a somewhat generalized plea for peace, which seems to exist hand in hand with the against-all-odds sense that peace has existed in the interim between the bombing and the moment we are talking in—all those other wars notwithstanding—and that it is their duty as a survivor to make sure that the people who died sacrificed their lives so we could have peace.

What struck me then: how they could forget so much; how they could make what they remembered so emotionless and dull? It is true that, in the aftermath of the bombing, during the Occupation, there was a crackdown on information about the effects of the bombs. Video and photographs were confiscated; reporters were tightly censored and kicked out of the country. But that political denial, as sweeping as it was, seemed pale when compared to the personal denial I was being offered.

It was a packaged story: what I was supposed to hear. It was the story of common experience, often told in the plural "we," in which people survived and helped each other, or died sacrificing themselves, and in either case accepted and endured. The result, although words were being spoken, was a great "sound of silence" about anything but peace.

It was honest; it was the truth. But it wasn't real.

I found out it wasn't real on September 12, 2001 when the interviews began to change. First there was shock, and then outrage, and then fear. The terrorist attacks in the U.S. splintered the narrative of Hiroshima, and the survivors' stories and memories wandered from their set paths—their minds wandered into forgotten territory, where they faltered, and became lost. They cried in front of me, a stranger, and remembered their loved ones who had died. Then, when the bombing of Afghanistan began, the uncertainty and hostility in the world unbalanced them, and there was anger too. And as they dredged up some very painful details of their lives, their faces held a look of surprise, shock even, that this was actually a piece of them—they were suddenly vulnerable, haunted by this awful experience that they had denied for so long.

One woman I spoke with, who was about eight at the time, told me about trying to fit her mother's eye back into its socket. Another remembered giving her child water and watching his lips attach and pull off onto the spout of the kettle. A man remembered cremating his two sons, age five and seven, and the fact that they didn't burn completely. "I never told my wife," he said. "It just wasn't something she could bear."

Memory is not history: memory is narrative, a way to rewrite personal experience, to rewrite self. The internment stories were full of that: of "forgetting" how to speak Japanese, of young men volunteering to fight even after being stripped of their citizenship—and, even more than that—of the first American generation helping to get their own parents and children "peaceably" interned.

The narrative of Hiroshima, of trauma, is also the narrative of rewritten self at its most basic level. It is requisite so that people can sleep at night. It was a way for them to transcend the shock, the disability, the shifts in their identity and even in their understanding of reality. If they could assign reasons for that bombing, and those reasons did not now exist, then they were safe.

Their goals, as people, were safety and healing.

But *our* goals as writers who want to explore the narratives of displacement, exile and trauma are the opposite. Not that we reject safety and healing, but that we are searching for remembrance. Once we get over being beguiled by research (facts are so protective!) and bedeviled by the issues of representation (there are always people who want to control any story, especially one that is little known, and who insist that only "one of us" can tell the story, and even then in only the most positive, politically correct way), we return to the question of how to create a true story from the narrative of forgetting.

First, we have to see their narrative for what it is: closure. It's not a lie, but it is some form of cover-up, since what it truly is is: the end. You can write <u>to</u> the end, or <u>from</u> the end, but you can't write only the end and try to make it all that happened.

To make your story come to life, and to be more than a report on what happened, you have to imagine your way into it. Here, the very thing that sets the narrative of the rewritten self apart—silence—is what will help you. Far from holding up the facts to say, "See, I know my stuff," you have to go to the scariest places, the absence, where nothing has been said so there is no protection at all.

These are places of fear. Theirs, and now yours. Rage; sorrow; the long, unbearable beat of helplessness: these are necessary in varying degrees depending on what form you are employing (creative nonfiction, memoir, fiction, poetry, dramatic writing). You must feel them, and claim them, in order to break the silence on the page. It would seem to be obvious, and it's contained in much of the craft advice we talk about: inhabit your characters; experience your story from the inside; write the story that is urgent to you; make it real, not factual. These can seem to be platitudes, touchy-feely but vague advice about which a student walks away from class saying—yeah, but how do I do that?

Stand in the absences. Fill in the blank space. Probe the places in the narrative where you just don't get it, or where you can feel a tension between what you would feel and what they say. This is not to say that you should enter a space that is entirely foreign to you and impose your contemporary American self (or however you think of yourself) on it. But you are a person and this, if it is worth telling, is a universal story. So something in it must speak to you. And will then speak through you.

It's as simple, and as difficult, and as necessary as that.

—*Delivered Winter, 2006, Plainfield, Vermont*

DRAWING THE LINE SOMEWHERE
By Richard Panek

During the final faculty meeting of the residency, we always discuss ideas for the theme of the following semester's residency. Last semester someone suggested "The Spirit of the Thing." The response around the table was instantaneous: *That's it!* The vote was swift and unanimous. Then we all laughed. We'd never seen such a response to a possible residency theme. A theme that, we might have noticed if we'd thought about it at all, consisted of two abstractions. If a student had written that phrase, any one of us would have scrawled "vague!" in the margin. I don't remember now who suggested "The Spirit of the Thing," but I doubt that she or he would have been able to say what it meant. I doubt that any of us could have said what those two nouns in that combination meant. But they sounded good together, and sometimes that's enough.

It was for me, anyway. Even as the program director asked if I would be one of the keynote speakers, I knew the topic I wanted to address. Another faculty member, Rachel Pollack, had invoked the Heisenberg uncertainty principle during her own keynote address that residency, and I'd been thinking about it all week—or near it, anyway: its less famous but, to my amateur-historian-of-science way of thinking, more profound corollary.

In early 1927, the German theorist Werner Heisenberg published a paper arguing that you can't make an observation at the quantum level without disturbing the object you're observing. (I'm summarizing broadly, both here and elsewhere in this essay.) All information comes to you from your senses, so if you wanted to observe an electron, for example, you would first have to find a way to make it accessible to sight. You would need a photon—a particle of light—to interact with it. That interaction, however, will disturb the electron under observation—the *thing*. We can observe the thing, but we have to change the thing in order to observe it, and that change leaves us at a loss: We can't describe the thing completely.

This insight provoked a crisis in physics that, as is often the case with upheavals in science, carried philosophical implications. Since the dawn of the Scientific Revolution three hundred years earlier, investigators of nature had proceeded under the assumption that if they wanted to describe a thing completely, they could do so. Now, suddenly, they knew they couldn't. The certainty that had sustained our interaction with nature, reality, the universe—whatever you wanted to call it— turned out to be, in retrospect, an illusion. What's a physicist to do?

Later that same year, the theorist Niels Bohr answered that question. In a lecture at the Como Conference in September 1927, he articulated a principle that expanded on Heisenberg's. True, he acknowledged, you can't describe a thing completely. On the quantum level you can't determine an electron's position and velocity simultaneously, for instance, or you can't invoke light as both particle and wave at the same time. But rather than interpreting the relationship between position and velocity or between particle and wave as contradictory, Bohr suggested, we might more profitably recast them as complementary. They're both correct; neither is complete. Light is a wave when we observe it one way; light is a particle when we observe it another way. The interaction between observer and the thing being observed not only disturbs the thing under observation but *defines* it

What's more, the definition should include not only the influence of the observer—the choice of particle or wave—but the conditions of the experiment. "When you ask, 'What is light?'" the historian of science Gerald Holton wrote about Bohr's complementarity, "the answer is: the observer, his various pieces and types of equipment, his experiments, his theories and models of interpretation, *and* whatever it may be that fills an otherwise empty room when the light bulb is allowed to keep on burning. All this, together, is light."

In an essay two years later, Bohr illustrated this idea by asking the reader to imagine using a stick to examine an object in a dark room (an illustration I'll take the liberty of extrapolating from). Where is the dividing line between you and the thing? Is it in the end of the stick as it prods the thing? The shaft of the stick as it bends or doesn't bend, vibrates or doesn't vibrate—as it becomes the vessel for the information that is passing from thing to you? Is it where your hand grips the other end of the stick? In the nerves that carry the information from the palm of your hand to your brain? In the neurons and synapses that create biological and chemical reactions that we interpret as information?

And then there's the thing. Where is the dividing line between it and its environment? Ever since Newton came up with the law of universal gravitation, physicists have assumed that matter attracts matter regardless of how far apart the two objects are. If the universe in its entirety consisted of two hydrogen atoms 10 billion light-years apart, they would still be gravitationally influencing each other. In principle, if you were defining the thing at the end of your stick, you would have to take into account the gravitational interaction between it and everything else.

This idea isn't as abstract or hypothetical as it might sound. I once visited a University of Washington laboratory where researchers had set up several experiments to test gravity. The laboratory was a concrete bunker, half-buried in the ground—the former site of a cyclotron. The principal investigator explained to me the gravitational factors he needed to take into account when calibrating the instruments. "There's metal here," he said, pointing to the various experiments. There's the ground water level in the soil on the other side of the wall, and it fluctuates every time it rains—which, this being Seattle, would mean a lot of fluctuation. "There's a hillside over here"—he waved a hand toward somewhere beyond the soil. "There's a lake over there"—waving his hand in another direction. And the effects aren't only local, he said. There's the rotation of the earth, the position of the sun, the dark matter in the halo of our galaxy.

And there's more. There always is. There's a whole universe out there, and if you don't set limits, then every consideration of the relationship between you and the thing would quickly deteriorate to the same reductionist conclusion: The thing is the universe. You have to draw the line somewhere—the line that isolates the system, that serves as its perimeter, that excludes everything in the universe that is not the thing. What you choose to include—what remains inside the perimeter, including you—is then by definition the thing.

And in some circumstances, we call that thing a book.

A novel. A collection of short stories. Your essay or screenplay, your poem or play. Over the decades, Bohr's examples of complementary relationships became more and more philosophical ("In the great drama of existence we are ourselves both actors and spectators"), and he found applications for the concept in "wider fields," far beyond physics—

psychology, biology, history, the arts. I don't think he would have objected to applying it to the act of writing—to the relationship between you the writer and that thing you've been working on.

Whatever you're writing, and at every moment you're writing it, you face a virtually infinite number of choices. You can choose among hundreds of thousands of words, you can put them in any order you wish, you can punctuate them senseless or sensible, you can break them up into chapters, stanzas, scenes, sections, lines, acts, paragraphs. And there's more. You have a universe of choices.

But you have to draw the line somewhere.

What Bohr wrote about experiments applies to writing as well: "The concept of observation is in so far arbitrary as it depends upon which objects are included in the system to be observed." The concept of the work-in-progress is in so far arbitrary as it depends upon which elements—words, punctuation, order, rhythm, and so on—you include in what you're writing.

Arbitrary, but not random. The choice of where to draw the line is quite deliberate. "When we look at the moon through a telescope," Bohr wrote, "we receive light from the sun reflected from the moon-surface, but the recoil from this reflection is far too small to have any effect on the velocity of a body as heavy as the moon." You have to take into account the effects of a collision between photon and electron, but you can safely choose to exclude from your observations the aftershock of a collision between photon and moon. The physicists doing the gravity experiments at the University of Washington do need to factor into their calibrations the rise in groundwater after a rainfall, but they don't need to take into account the gravitational tug of a hydrogen atom 10 billion light-years away. Somewhere between those two extremes they draw the line. And where they draw the line defines the thing—the thing that is the relationship between them and what they seek to measure, in its totality.

"When anybody asks what a story is about, the only proper thing is to tell him to read the story," Flannery O'Connor once wrote. "A story is something that can't be said any other way, and it takes every word in the story to say what the meaning is." I would go further, and she would have, too, I suspect. Every word affects the meaning, but so does every piece of punctuation, every paragraph break. With each of those choices the line you draw around the work-in-progress shifts. Each addition to or subtraction from the text—each interaction between you the writer and the thing you're creating—alters what is within the perimeter and what is not, what is part of the work and what is not. It redefines the thing.

Like the notion of gravitational attraction across unfathomable distances, the idea that the tiniest edit affects the entirety of a work is not as abstract or hypothetical as it might sound. A piece of writing lives and dies by how rigorously it adheres to its definition of itself—by how astutely the writer chooses what to place on either side of the line. The kind of work that Flannery O'Connor was referring to—the story that defies summation—would be one where you can't understand the meaning of a word or a comma without knowing its context: its adjoining words, its sentence, its paragraph, and so on, until you have a universe. Not the whole universe. But the universe of the story: the thing in the dark room that you the writer have defined by where you have chosen to draw the line.

The thing—this object that you have created, this written work—is not complete in itself. In the complementarity interpretation, the thing is both you, the writer, plus the thing you're working on. And soon the thing will also be we, the readers, plus the thing. Which raises a question: What do we even mean by "thing" if it is writer-plus-thing, or reader-plus-thing, or writer-plus-reader-plus-thing, and all of the above? What is this thing that is thing-plus? Words fail us—another favorite topic of Bohr's.

So let's do what Bohr did and concede that we're stuck with the limitations of a language that evolved to describe a pre-quantum world. Let's say the thing is what you might naïvely but understandably think is the thing: novel, poem, play, keynote address. In that case, this other thing—the relationship between thing and writer, between thing and reader, between writer and reader: the totality of the experience: *thing-plus*—is what we might call, in language less abstract and hypothetical and "vague!" than it might at first seem, the spirit of the thing.

—Delivered Summer, 2010, Plainfield, Vermont

WHAT'S HELD INSIDE
By Elena Georgiou

After the last planning meeting for this residency I had to keep repeating the theme—*The Spirit of the Thing, The Spirit of the Thing*—as if it were a mantra, because this was the only way I could hang onto the words.

Later that day, in the cafeteria, I asked various faculty members if they could tell me what it meant, and one of them was kind enough to attempt an explanation by pointing to the saltshaker on the table and saying, "It means something like if you are going to write about this saltshaker, well, it wouldn't simply be about the saltshaker, but the spirit of the saltshaker."

In that moment, I *did* have a fleeting understanding; but then ten seconds passed and I was back to thinking: What exactly is a saltshaker's spirit? And if it exists, how will I find it? I will return to the spirit of a saltshaker in minute. For now, I will say that at the time I was sure this residency theme was doomed.

And then a few months passed, and I sat down to write this keynote. This was when instead of repeating the words, I questioned *why* it was that I could not hang onto to them. Was it the theme itself? No, it wasn't *that* because I still didn't know what it actually meant. In attempting to jot down some notes, I came to the conclusion that this particular grouping of words—*the spirit of the thing*—flies in the face of everything that my own writing strives to be. The only words that aren't completely generic—*spirit* and *thing*—are completely abstract, and in my own writing world the use of abstractions is the biggest crime I can commit. If I can't touch, taste, smell, hear, or see any of the words, then, for me, there is no magic, no mystery at work. If the words *spirit* and *thing* are in the first draft of something I've written, I circle them and make a notation to immediately replace these abstractions with something specific— something that will hopefully make my readers' bodies open to allow my words to enter. And in replacing these abstractions with something specific I also hope to show my readers that I wrote the poem—that it has my signature attached to it. The spirit of whatever *thing* I am describing—be it a saltshaker or Lemon Verbena petals—has to make my reader pay attention to the exact choice of words I'm using to compose the images, as well as highlighting how I have chosen to speak about the specific idea.

So let's return to the saltshaker in the cafeteria for a second. If that saltshaker has a spirit, then how do I find it? The *actual* saltshaker I was directed toward is a relatively non-descript white, plastic thing that holds a substance that is precious, but is mostly taken for granted, unless something out of the ordinary happens to it. And it just so happens that something unusual did happen to one of the white saltshakers in the cafeteria.

One morning during the last residency, a woman on the cleaning staff told me that she came into the cafeteria, and on the table was the ghost of an old man in coveralls sitting in a rocking chair. He began rocking and then he reached down to pick up the saltshaker, poured a little salt into his palm and tossed it over his shoulder.

"What did you do when you saw him?" I asked.

"Nothing. I just couldn't understand why he had his rocker on the table. It would have been scary enough if he had it on the floor. And when he began tossing the salt over his shoulder, I was surprised that ghosts also believed in bad luck. Then the old man and his rocker disappeared, and all that was left was the mess he made with the salt, and I went over to clean it up. But when I got close I saw the saltshaker was not the same; it had melted slightly, and instead of its previously smooth sides, it had molded into the ghost's grip. There it was, on the table, with indentations where there had once been ghostfingers. Weird," she said.

"Yeah, weird," I said.

So there you have it—my story to illustrate the *spirit of the thing*. But wait. That's not right, is it? Is this the spirit *of* the thing or is it the spirit *and* the thing? Well, this story is about what happened to the salt-shaker on the *outside*, not what happened to it on the *inside*, where its spirit is supposed to reside. Therefore, I don't think this story is what the planners of this residency meant when they came up with this theme. So let me try again.

Perhaps, among us, there are writers who do not believe in the kind of spirit that is a ghost in overalls who sits on a cafeteria table. What would the *spirit* of the *thing* mean for them?

To answer this question, I would like us to think about something I'm guessing about 95% of us believe in, and that is a *thing* called *love*. Love is both simultaneously invisible and visible. For example: My mother loves me. She really, really, loves me. I've written it. This is a clear, direct, simple sentence that contains a truthful and believable piece of information, information I am now offering to you. And because I have written it, and I am telling you the truth, you believe me. You do believe me, don't you? You're not sure? Well, let's see: Are you moved by what I've told you about my mother's love for me? Not really? Why not? Because nothing about these words is evocative, memorable, and magical? Because I haven't given you the *spirit of the thing* called *love*.

So let me try again: When I was a child my mother collected Lemon Verbena petals from our garden, dried them in her bedroom closet, and put them inside my pillowcase so that Lemon Verbena was the first thing I smelled when I woke each morning. What do you think about my mother's relationship to me now? Have I evoked love? Do you believe that my mother loves me? You do? Is it because I have infused Lemon Verbena petals with the spirit of my mother's love? Is it because your body tries to smell the Lemon Verbena? Is it because your body tries to feel the cotton pillowcase against your cheek? Is it because your body tries to remember what it was like to wake up from a childhood sleep? Is it because in offering you an emblematic image from my childhood, it makes you go into yourself to think about your own? Is it because even though you've never met my mother, and even though your mother did not do this exact same thing to show her love for you, you still see and feel the spirit of my mother's love?

But what if I told you that my childhood home was actually an apartment above a liquor store, and instead of a garden the store had a parking lot; and in this parking lot there was no Lemon Verbena for my mother to collect, dry, and put inside my pillowcase? What if I told you that instead of waking to a citrusy smell, I used to wake up to a silent house that smelled of damp wood; that I crept downstairs, avoiding the steps that creaked because my mother was still asleep and she hated mornings and I would try my best not to wake her up? And what if I told you that each morning, I had the same routine: I soft-boiled an egg, broke off the top, and poked my spoon into the yolk? Then, without lifting my head from the book I was reading, I would reach for the souvenir from my parent's honeymoon—a beige, mushroom-shaped saltshaker—and I would sprinkle the salt into my egg. This beige and silent vessel sat on the kitchen table for years; and even though we took it for granted, we also knew it held something precious inside.

So now you have two mothers, two childhoods. Is it the mushroom-shaped saltshaker or the petals in the pillowcase that carries the spirit of my childhood? I am hoping that you cannot tell, that my words have done what they were supposed to do—engage you with vivid images that make you feel the *spirit* of each *thing* I have described.

Here's the answer: The Lemon Verbena petals in the pillowcase hold the spirit of a mother's love. This mother does not belong to me; she belongs to an undergraduate student I taught approximately 15 years ago. Sadly, I have forgotten this student's name, and I feel bad about this, since I always use this particular image of a mother's love to give an example of how an image can be emblematic, idiosyncratic, specific, and still be universal. This image has been with me all these years, because part of me cannot believe there is such a mother in the world, a mother so different from my own. It doesn't matter that I have had no experience with this mother. The spirit of her love placed inside dried petals, placed inside a pillowcase, evokes everything I need to infuse this abstraction of "love" with spirit.

When I think of my childhood, its spirit is beige and silent. The image of a saltshaker to represent it came to me because of my introduction to this keynote. Somewhere in my memory I hold an image of a beige mushroom-shaped saltshaker from some English, working-class, seaside town. It is a vague image. I can barely see it. But I know that my parents' honeymoon was a few days in a seaside town called Torquay. So I took this vague image of a mushroom-shaped saltshaker and imagined that my parents had bought it on their honeymoon and put it on the kitchen table, years before I came along. And there it remained, beige and silent.

Once I placed it on the kitchen table of my imagination, my childhood mornings became concrete. Like a mushroom, I was growing in a dark, damp place, and like this saltshaker I was quiet, but I held something valuable inside.

So now that I've almost come to the end of this keynote and now that I've revealed the truth of which childhood belongs to me, I'm imagining that you are now wondering about the other saltshaker in this piece—the one in the hands of the ghost on the cafeteria table. Well, let's see... What do you know for sure? That there are white plastic saltshakers on the cafeteria tables. That the cleaning staff does clean the dormitories and the cafeteria. That this college campus has ghosts that live with us mortals. (Well, okay, maybe some of us don't believe in the ghosts...) So what's the "truth" for *this* spirit and *this* thing? Here it is: A woman on the cleaning staff did tell this story, but not to me. She told it to my partner who was dropping me off at a residency. And it wasn't she who saw the ghost but one of her co-workers—a man on the maintenance staff. And the ghost was indeed sitting in a rocking chair on top of the table, but he did not have a saltshaker in his hand, he did not toss salt over his shoulder, and, therefore, the maintenance man did not witness the melted sides of the plastic saltshaker after the ghost disappeared. This was a flourish from yours truly to give this vignette a bit of extra seasoning and spice.

In my beige childhood, I always wanted to give my world sensuality and seasoning, and I did this by recognizing the *spirit* in every *thing* that surrounded me—the spoon, the eggcup, each damp, creaking step. I might have been a quiet child, but that didn't stop me from feeling that just about everything was waiting for me to see it, to bring it to life. And what has remained true from childhood into adulthood is that I feel as if all *things* already have *spirits* before I come along to notice them, and a great part of my job as a writer is to see everything, to never take the *spirit* of any *thing* for granted, and to remember that each word I use holds a spirit inside.

—*Delivered Summer, 2010, Plainfield, Vermont*

DEAR WRITER
By Kyle Bass

Dear Writer,

Over the course of your graduate study here at Goddard you have received no fewer than 20 letters from your advisors in response to your work. The pages of all those letters, each one freighted, I'm sure, with wisdom, patience, challenge and encouragement, amount to a forever-giving textbook, a patient guide written exclusively for you. What I have for you today is an afterword to that book, those letters—some reminders, things you ought not to forget as you float out these doors, away from this campus and into the rest of your life, your life as a writer.

First, remember that your creative thesis, written in your time at Goddard, is perhaps the very thing you thought you could never or would never complete. You did. But don't allow yourself to feel that you are done, not in any way. You're not. Remember that you've only just started and that you'll always be a kind of beginner. Each new blank page will remind you of that, should you forget.

And even with the potential its pages both promise and already fulfill, more than your creative thesis—newly born and resting now at Pratt Library, on the other side of the fairy-tale stand of trees over there, down that enchanting-by-day and a-little-scary-by-night path—and even more than the MFA degree, which I know has cost you a pretty little penny and perhaps some piece of your love life or marriage—remember this: the thing of true value you take away from Goddard is the *habit of a writer*. And that, *the habit of a writer*—not the fish but the fishing and the fishing again—is all you really have, is all you will ever have upon which to build and sustain your writer's life; it is from within that you will begin and eventually deliver your next work, and the one after that, and the one after that, and the one after... But there's a catch: Free of what one of my colleagues calls "the unnatural strictures" of this program, its packet due dates and deadlines, I'm afraid, dear Writer, you're on your own. Welcome to the club. Remember to pay your dues.

Remember that the habit of a writer embraces the habit of absence, self-imposed exile, "the aloneness," wrote James Baldwin, "in which one discovers that life is tragic and therefore unutterably beautiful." Remember to be absent, Writer. Be in the habit of being absent more often. As a character in the play *Inventing Van Gogh* reminds us, Van Gogh didn't paint a portrait of Gauguin; Van Gogh made a painting of Gauguin's chair, a portrait of the artist in absence.

Remember that it's in your aloneness that you're most able to search out words, forms and structures, to discover and sharpen your instruments of expression, to utter, somehow, the unutterable, the beautiful, the truth of being alive and human and stunned, in awe of life's woes and wonders. And please, dear Writer, in this troubled world, remember to bring life's wonders into your work.

And alone with your writing, where there is no world but the one you fashion, remember to let slip or pry off the mask, because writing that's worth anyone reading won't, never has and never will emerge from your mask. Remember that. Maybe save your mask and all its beautiful lies for your day job, and for your neighbors, and for dinner parties. However you do it, remember to keep something of yourself *for* yourself alone. For to give it *all* away leaves you with nothing, barren, searching an empty tomb when it comes time to write, to wake your dead.

When your advisors urged you to "go deeper" with your writing, remember that this was what we meant: No bullshit. Not one word of it. Bullshit is the language of the mask. And no skimming the surface of what you mean, what you feel, what you fear, what you love, what you hate, what you think you know or what you don't. No writerly posing allowed in the writers' pool where, you'll recall, each end is the deep end. Bullshit is a flotation device; write holes through it. Remember to go deep, dive, sink and get lost under the waves, beneath the ice. Remember to muddy the waters.

Like all art, writing must, I think, finally be your deepest most honest response to the allure of the truth, the terrible truth, the beautiful truth. And remember that the truth is always the truth of yourself. Use your aloneness, your exile, to conjure absence and its offspring longing, for in absence and longing we find, I think, the beginning of truth, we set foot upon the first stones of the path toward truth.

Don't worry about being original. We are all influenced, remember? Your writing has roots in the past. "Everything great," said Goethe, "molds us from the moment we become aware of it." Just remember to write *your* truth and it *will be* original. It might even be great. "The important thing," said Georgia O'Keefe, "is to make your unknown known." Remember those words.

An acclaimed young writer who let nearly eleven years pass between his first book and his second once said, "The happiest person in the world is a writer not writing." Yeah, I get it but I don't buy it, and neither should you. So don't remember that. Remember this instead: Hard as it is, it's best to feed your habit, Writer, even if it kills you. You'll be happier if you do. So, nurse it, or be its whore. Remember: whatever it takes! Fit your life into your writing, not the other way around. And don't worry: those who love you, love Writer-you, will forgive you your habitual disappearing act. If not, then find better lovers, or remember to dedicate your next manuscript to someone else! Initials are always good: "*To J.C.—happy to be left alone so I can write.*"

If you recall that in a letter or in a workshop I've said to you, "Write with neither hope nor despair," remember that I was speaking in ideal terms, my wishful thinking for you, to forestall the inevitable. What I think you will discover—if you haven't already, you will if you keep at it—is that the writer's life is a slurry of dread, desperation and discipline. Remember to hold fast to discipline; practice letting go of desperation. Dread you will find is for keeps.

Remember that it takes fortitude, guts and balls to be a writer. Writing will never be easy but it does get easier to bear and sometimes transcend its difficulty, as is almost always the case when we exercise discipline well.

When you're writing you're *kind* of special, but when you're not writing you're mostly like everyone else: You want to be wanted, liked, lusted after, loved, remembered. These mortal needs, oh, how they do creep into the work. We want to be read and thought well of, especially early on and, I'm told, near the end of a writing life and, likewise, early on and near the end of a draft of a new work. I know the feeling. Hidden away on my computer are the early drafts, the picked-over ruins of this very commencement address, begun in a quiet terror, I admit, out of my desire, my desperation for you to think me wise and worthy of this honor. But as I wrote, as happens the more I write, the hope that it be good and the despair that it will never be good enough fell away, leaving me by myself, in my study, at what had been my father's desk, alone with my chaos of thoughts and memory of order. Eventually, with hope and despair in retreat, I was no longer writing *for you*, dear Writer, I was writing *because of you*—you, my inspiration.

Master the habit of putting your butt in your writing chair on a regular basis and inspiration, that whispered rumor of beauty, will visit more often; no, not when you call for it, and not when you make a communion of another drink, or another cigarette, or another box of shortbread cookies, or scream, or pray, or cry, or (and this I stole from Faulkner) *howl with human reason*. Inspiration ain't your bitch like that! Inspiration ain't nobody's dog! Inspiration doesn't come when you call! Inspiration is the unpredictable, *unsummonable* reward for *being there* at your writing table, through all the uninspired hours, there to greet its sudden arrival and host its brief stay. The writer's habit is the habit of being there to make something of that reward, the surprising and demanding gift of inspiration, which delivers the thing craft alone could not invent.

Think of your time at Goddard as your inspiration. Better yet, think of your time at Goddard as your training to *respond to* inspiration. At least 20 process letters, no less than 45 annotations, two short critical papers, one long critical paper, a teaching practicum and essay, a process paper, final paperwork, and finally your creative thesis! At least 20 x 40 packet pages...remember that? The space *that* work required is the same space that must now hold (and fail to contain) all your own work. That's the brilliance and gift of this program. Please, don't ever forget that.

Success is sweet but don't be too charmed by its outside-the-writing-room promises. Pretty and validating as they are, publication, readers, productions, audiences, agents, accolades and awards must not be your aim when you sit down to write and before your work is done. Remember to be passionate about discipline and the process and your craft. And remember that your first draft is not your story, book, screenplay, play or poem; your first draft is you *discovering* your story, book, screenplay, play, or poem. So, write, rewrite, and write some more. To hell with the reader and the audience. It's not for them now, not yet. Ignore the temptation, when the going gets tough, to start something new. It's just a draft. Laugh at your own jokes. Cry when you hit a nerve. And remember to enjoy it. Deny yourself nothing. Indulge your every whim. Roll in your lowest standards, happy as a pig in poop, but remember, as a poet once said, to *keep in your soul some image of magnificence* too. Your high standards will be there when you need them. So bang those keys! Make some noise! Make music of your words. What appeals to the ear stays in the mind. Pound rhythms into your keyboard! Make your truth sing! Remember your passion for the work, the process, and let the rest take care of itself. You've done it once and perhaps before. The only thing left is to do it again and again and again...

And remember to forget anything I've said here if it gets in the way of your work.

This is where I bid you good luck and this is where I say, formally, Goodbye from Goddard. Hurts a little, doesn't it? I know... I remember. But I hope you will take this as a salve: I love you. I love you in the work you've done to get to this day, and I love you in the writing you will do—if you do, *I hope you do*—in all your days to come.

Dear Writer: your gift is yours to do with what you will. So write and, as Carlos Fuentes reminds us to do, "Invent what the world lacks, what the world has forgotten, what it hopes to attain and perhaps can never reach." And never stop. Never give up. Never ever break this habit and you will have truly mastered something.

Congratulations... All the best...

Write soon.

—*Delivered Summer, 2010, Plainfield, Vermont*

II. COMPOSING THE WILDERNESS

THE FREAK IN ALL OF US
(or the importance of creating a map)
By Rogelio Martinez

Writers are freaks. We are. You are a freak. I'm a freak. He's a freak. We all are.

Okay, maybe not completely. But they—meaning the general population—think we are. Why? One question that writers are always asked: *How long did it take you to write the story?*

It's as if we're this special being that retreats into some room—a Noah John Rondeau, the famous hermit of Appalachia—only to come out every so often to show off our writing.

What should we do when confronted with such a question? Three choices:

1. Tell the truth and reveal the long winding road that is the map of the work

2. Give some kind of glib response that's partially true.

3. Lie.

The truth will bore your audience quickly. Try talking about drafts and outlines and workshops and feedback and mapping the work, and you will lose your genius status very quickly. We don't want to do that.

A glib response is like the one that John Guare, Tony Award winning playwright of *The House of Blue Leaves*, gave when he was asked how long it took him to write *Six Degrees of Separation*: It took three weeks, or 51 years (his age at the time he wrote the play). It's a nice response. But after you hear it several times it becomes too neat, maybe even shallow. It's as if John has been preparing 51 years to answer that question. It's as if he had the answer ready before he even wrote the play. There's no spontaneity.

Now with that in mind we arrive at lying. Lying is always more interesting because it becomes a kind of story in and of itself. It's not the right thing to do; lying never is. However, keep in mind that your audience/reader is not doing the right thing by asking you how long it took you to write the work. They should be complimenting you. They should be showering you with praise. Buying you steak dinners (my apologies to vegetarians).

Their question makes lying almost necessary. Here is what I mean by that. What if you tell them the truth, you tell them that it only took you a week to write a three hundred page novel? Does it make it worse, or better in their eyes? What do you think? What if someone reads a book of yours, gives it a C+, then finds out it took you ten years to write it, and they bump up that C+ to a solid B. Oh, they will. That's how they think. The reader often equates quality with time. John Guare knew that, so he gave the glib response. He wanted to tell the truth BUT wanted the audience to like him...to like his play. Three weeks. Fifty-one years.

So is there a reason to tell the truth and reveal the map? Why should we give the reader an atlas to the soul of our work? Why should we be honest with our audience? Why should we reveal the scaffolding that holds up the work instead of just the work itself?

The answer, I think, is rather simple. Writing is difficult work. Without a map we may make it through the woods the first time around on instinct, but to have a career, a real sustaining career, we have to map the work so that we don't get lost the next time. Create a map of the roads travelled so that can we discover new roads. Lie or give a glib response, and we're going to start to believe what we're saying. Eventually we will get lost in a mess of a play or a book.

I began by referring to freaks, which was my own personal tribute to Ray Bradbury's wonderfully inventive and at times richly melancholic *The Illustrated Man*. The book begins in Wisconsin in the summer. The narrator meets a man claiming to have been kicked out of every carnival job he's had. Basically the guy is covered in illustrations, unemployed, and looking for some company. The illustrations are little stories that predict the future and at night come to life. The Illustrated Man is not happy with his fate. He feels the burden of being a storyteller. As the two turn in for the night, the stories begin.

We are all Illustrated Men and Women looking for a carnival to hire us. Our bodies are covered with stories. And there's no doubt in my mind that when that gas bill is due, we have all felt the burden of being Illustrated. We are marked for life. No doubt great things will happen to us, terrible things will come visiting, but we have lived unique enough lives that our bodies are walking stories. To map the work we only examine ourselves.

How long does it take to write a play? I'm starting to think that John Guare had it partly right. It takes a lifetime to write a play. With this in mind, I'm going to share 38 years worth of maps. It's not going to take 38 years. It's not going to take 38 minutes. Give me 3.8 minutes.

Born in Sancti Spiritus, Cuba, to an engineer and a teacher. Nine years later I leave the country in the Mariel boatlift. My father stays behind because he is not allowed to go.

On my body the images begin to appear. Kissing my father goodbye. My grandmother washing the graffiti off the side of the house as we say goodbye. Watching my mother, dressed to the nines, thinking the trip to the United States will be an easy one. The boat I'm on—the *TwoBill*—swaying back and forth in rough waters—people throwing up. A sign in Key West: "Last person to Leave Cuba, please turn off the lights." We're disembarking now. Marines are waiting for us at the bottom. They have cans of Coca-Cola with the tabs. No one knows how to open them. The refugees are now in small groups, little gangs of immigrants trying to figure out how to open their cans.

The stories begin to shape themselves.

Fizz is my wild retelling of Roberto Goizueta's time as CEO of the Coca-Cola Company. Goizueta, a refugee like myself, went on to introduce the incredibly successful Diet Coke and...drum roll please... the equally disastrous New Coke. Goizueta was a foreigner, so this helped him have no reverence for the company. Believe it or not, it was a big deal among Coca-Cola bigwigs to put a word in front of Coke, Diet in front of Coke. The image of a Coca-Cola can on my body brings to life a play.

Here on my left arm is an illustration. I'm trying to figure out why I write about Cuba when I only spent nine years there. The play is *Arrivals and Departures*. Two brothers compete for the title of being the real voice of Cuba. One writer stayed behind and is the darling of the Revolution, one writer left and is the darling of Hollywood. I'm the darling of neither but here I am wrestling with my identity.

On my neck you can see my play *Learning Curve*. African-Americans are taking over the Cornell campus in the late 60s. This is the breakthrough play for me. It's not my best play, but it's the most daring. With *Learning Curve* I'm stepping outside of my comfort zone and no longer writing about Cubans. I struggle with the idea that it's not my right to tell this story about African Americans, but soon enough I see the similarities. I draw on my own experiences in college. Words, images, and meaning fight their way to the page. The play becomes a kind of learning curve. After I finish it, I feel that I can write about anything.

Here on my forehead is an image of my cousin Ricardito teaching me how to say my very first word in English. The word is "ok." He would die of AIDS on June 8th, 1987 at the age of 28. The story begins to take shape. A teenager abandoned by his mother writes the very first computer virus while his unsuspecting father deals with the AIDS crisis at work. My play *Elk Cloner* is a story about viruses destroying lives.

I promised you 3.8 minutes—a kind of countdown. I have long been fascinated with countdowns. Here on my chest you can see the nine-year-old boy looking at Columbia taking off for the first time. Here on my right leg you can see a sixteen-year-old boy walking into French class only to learn that the Challenger has crashed. Here I am a man writing about the space shuttle program and the International Space Station in my play *When Tang Met Laika*. 5.4.3.2.1.

The work is a map with roads and highways connecting the different sections of my body. I never write one play about one subject. I usually write three plays about one subject, each play getting closer to the soul of the work. Therefore, my maps are full of dead ends and false starts. Workshops that lead back to the drawing board, notes that lead me down a road that hasn't been plowed. Plays that lead me down hills to valleys rich with material. Each play, each illustration, shows up on several parts of my body. Each illustration slightly different than the next.

I have the maps, but what is my compass? Curiosity. Curiosity becomes the means by which I move through my writing world. I don't map the work as much as I map the road that leads me to the highway which leads me to the rest stop (or as we playwrights call it, intermission).

From there I get back on the highway and take the only exit that makes sense. I don't know where I'm going, but I do have the experience of having gone down the wrong road before.

It is a year now since Harold Pinter died, but I remember reading an interview with Mel Gussow in which he discussed *Betrayal*. Pinter said that his desire to move backwards in time, rather than forward, did not come from any kind of trickery but rather from the need to know what had occurred in these characters' lives. He knew something big had happened and he just needed to move backwards to find out. Pinter didn't map out his plays. He went searching for them. He followed roads most of us are uncomfortable following. "I find at the end of the journey, which of course is never ending, that I have found things out."

—Delivered Summer, 2009, Plainfield, Vermont

WORKS CITED:

Bradbury, Ray. *The Illustrated Man.* New York: HarperCollins Publishers Inc. 1953. Print.

Guare, John. *Six Degrees of Separation.* New York: Vintage Books. 1994. Print.

James, Henry. *The Pension Beaurepas.* Kindle Edition. Electronic.

Martinez, Rogelio. *Arrivals and Departures.* New York: Broadway Play Publishing. 2006. Print.

–. "Learning Curve." *New Playwrights: The Best Plays of 2005.* Ed. D.L. Lepidus. New York: Smith and Krauss. 2005. Print.

Pinter, Harold. *Betrayal.* New York: Grove/Atlantic Inc. 1978. Print.

MAPPING THE DARK WORLD

By Bhanu Kapil

I'd intended to write a brief talk on the post-colonial map: the fact that it's not possible to say the word for map without repeating the one for war. Cartography[,] I wanted to write[,] as played out for two hundred years or more, in the sentence as written in English[,] functions[:] as an intensely smooth line. Consider: the long-distance surface travel required of the map artist; his articulate and constantly enriched record that ensured the line, in time, would become a groove. A groove then a prediction. A fate then a colony. A colony then a weird border superimposed upon nomadic, religious or agricultural flows already present. I refer you to the contested borders of India, Israel, Ireland, and Iraq. I refer you to the sentence, the line that ends the poem, as a possible record of land expropriation, of the kind of liminal, historical space that appears whenever one territory is over-written by another. I might refer you to the "reach" (Renee Gladman) of the line as it appears in emergent forms, the contemporary value of a complex and abundant accumulation of images and details. You know this book, you know this line, and I don't know how else to say it, because I don't write fluently, or even passably, to tell the truth, in an alternate language, but I want it to leave. I want the English to leave.

In fact, they did leave, and without the option or desire to become an immigrant in reverse, to take up writing epic poems in rudimentary Punjabi or French, I find myself trying to work out the problem of the page, of the language and images I use to fill it, in a way that also embeds or mimics a history of "awards" and their subsequent carnage. Boundary awards, as the British described them when they "pulled out," which is risky post-coital [colonial] behavior at the best of times. I ran this by a poet, Thom Donovan, in the comments section of Harriet, the Poetry Foundation blog, a couple of days before coming to the residency. He replied: "your commentary reminds me of Benjamin's phrase, that there is no cultural artifact which does not exist as a record of barbarism. only here—in terms of the sentence—it is a grammar/punctuation which records barbarities. it is interesting that you locate this barbarity in the sentence. the period definitely serves a regulatory function, and it is interesting how non-Anglocentric Englishes respond to this nomos. trace the deformation of the sentence/syntax in American lit. and one will discover lines of flight away from Anglo(phono)centrism. was English always an enclosure, a potential border for mercantile-belligerence? does the period itself enclose? can a grammar be non-expropriational/commoning?"

There's something here, in Thom's extraordinary remarks, about a radical re-mapping or diagramming of space as one way to get this strange work (writing) done: the visual practice of holding the old map up the light until its marks evaporate or, like nodes, slip off onto the floor. Don't slip. Don't slip in that pool of blood. And though this appeals to me as an experimental writer, as a person engaged with the possibilities of cross-genre forms, it doesn't help me with what I'm writing about. It doesn't help me with the actual effects of crossing, from one space to another: displacement, diaspora, or what it feels like in the body to begin again. How it feels, fifty years later. And what if you can't. What if you can't find a fixed place on the map, which is a definition of shelter that precedes, let's say, mental health. Citizenship. Sex. If not sex, then the sense, in a community, of being known to others, touched lightly in passing: that most basic of proprioceptive acts. The smile. The pat. The shake.

Mapping this kind of psycho-social space, I turn to the writing of the Nigerian poet and novelist, Chris Abani, who was here at Goddard three or four residencies ago saying fabulous things about architecture and Korean horror movies. In the current issue of Oakland's *Tea Party Magazine*, he writes: "The difficulty for me is always, how do you frame these difficult subjects—war, grave incest and abuse, cannibalism, whatever it is—without creating sensationalism, but at the same time, without avoiding the harder details? How does that then turn into something that can be transformative, so it's not just a pornographic reproduction of violence as titillation but rather a kind of visceral-ness that forces ritual to happen? [So] it's not just the subject matter but that there is a collapse between the reader and the subject...and when you're reading the work, its happening to your body—it's not happening to the character's body." Later in this essay/interview, Abani suggests that writing from a place beyond the given or received map, America versus what he calls the continent, is how he builds the distance, the necessary voice or view, that allows him to engage a subject matter without "responding to it as an immediate threat."

It helps to find the edge of the map, and to exit. But what if you were born in a country that no longer exists? What if you were born in a country that did not recognize you as a citizen, legally or with your ethnic mark? What if leaving one map went well, but arriving in the next one did not? What if there was no shelter? No community? No health care? What if the effects of a borderland dispute were played out not on land, not as terrorist acts, but in a domestic future scene: the high incidence of domestic violence and mental illness in Caribbean and Asian communities in north-west London, with relational effects in the second generation, is a quick, dull and interesting example. See: Dinesh Bhugra's excellent *Cross-Cultural Psychiatry*, with its mutating diagrams of migration, stress, race, and somatic results of all kinds.

Writing these notes for this panel, I realize that I've got it all wrong, but it's too late to write a new talk. A diasporic map is not the same as a post-colonial map in its first minutes or years. The diasporic map is not working just with space, but with time; and as such, it requires a new technology to select, record and transcribe not the sentence, not the unobstructed forward-moving line, already problematized in contemporary writing as the question of movement and what impedes it—but what the sentence contains. What's foregrounded as an act in this other kind of map is our intersection with movement—only possible when it awkwardly stabilizes—when the bleeping red dot stops moving across the screen. This relation then is vertical—a sort of homing in upon a molecular speck of immigrant matter, which has stilled enough to let you see. Being volatile, it blurs, recedes and so on, and so this mapping technology must take account of micro and macro processes—weather patterns, neighborhood growth and depletion, the time of day —and so on.

A map I've already worked with, in my project *Schizophrene*, is a GIS map of London—a satellite map that is programmed to over-lay or stack information from social, legal and psychiatric databases. A map of specific ethnic minorities is overlapped with a Social Services map of homes recorded as being rented or owned by adults with schizophrenia or schizo-affective disorders; this in turn is overlapped with a map of emergency calls to police with reports of domestic violence or other acts of physical abuse that took place within a home. The person reading this map sees the nodes where a particular house flares. It spills an indigo or dark blue cloud into the grid. The grid is the silvery-grey background, what we typically call a map. But what I'm looking at is map-like in its rendering of an image that's exceeded its capacity to withhold or bear what it's got inside. For the first time, I find something on a map that resembles the body I am trying to write about. The schizophrenic. The immigrant. The sentence that won't stop, just as a certain kind of speech does not hesitate. A color that ruptures and starts to leak, attracting the attention of passers-by, riveting them to the spot. Someone's hit. Someone screams.

Mapping the work from above, I see the schizophrenic herself has started to vibrate, a vibration that extends to the texture and structure of her "shelter"—the house. Thus, instead of describing a character or a figure, the work is now to notate, so to speak, a disseminated "red and black." A kind of blue. My question for this project becomes, via Abani's call to transform the conditions as they are, and not just to claim them: How do I compose/re-compose a body that's pure sensation? Is it ethical to use the vertical line, to scrape color and light into a jar, at the expense of the horizontal one, the narrative that records arrival in its many forms?

Edward Said, in the years before his death, combined "reflections on exile" with those on music, building a language for resonance that interestingly overlapped post-colonial tropes, though Said never makes that explicit. "Atonality," suggested Said, prefigures an integrated phrase or key, or the desire for one. Studying his reading of a chaotic yet magnetized line, or set of lines, perhaps I can propose, too, that the transformative capacity of the GIS map is its ability to "hold" or briefly observe vibratory effects of the sort I've described above: a loss of form and release of color that's primal, intense and completely real in its entanglement of different layers and saturated points. The map that makes visible what was not visible, or audible, before. The map as a precursor to the body.

What this looks like for me, as a basic writing practice, is a magnified relationship with my notebooks or first drafts, which I scan for fragments, phrases or lines that "entangle," "flare," or "burst." Translating this geo-political view of terrain to the page has become a profound pleasure. Architecture, event and geology coincide, in what is map-like, to make use of the map in a new way. Here are a few new questions that I hope to bring to the exchanges with my students, here at Goddard, in the coming months; I invite you to answer them too:

1. How will you program your map? What social, political, or environmental databases could you use?

2. If the map is an imaging technology, then how does it function both as telescope and microscope? How do we select the thing we want to see?

3. When was the last time you opened then re-folded a paper map?

4. A map is a decision someone makes, not an entity. Is this true?

5. Write a sentence that attracts. How?

—*Delivered Winter, 2010, Plainfield, Vermont*

COMPOSING THE WILDERNESS
By Ryan Boudinot

Fifty-five miles north of Seattle, just off Interstate 5, on a seven-acre tract of land that included a pasture, two ponds, and a forest contiguous with dozens more acres of woodland, was my childhood home. For decades the previous owners of our property had used one of the ponds as a garbage dump, tossing appliances, household trash, and dairy farm equipment down the hill beyond a rowdy patch of rhododendrons. For thirty years my father cleaned up the property, making frequent trips to the garbage dump and clearing swaths of brush, which he piled in great mounds and delightedly set ablaze. I played in the overgrown ruins, digging through layers of moss and underbrush to unearth glass bleach bottles, cutlery, ceramic cold cream containers, spools of barbed wire, even the hood of a Mercedes Benz. I stashed these treasures in an old Darigold refrigerated train car which I referred to as my "lab," where we also kept hay for our sheep. I spent summers eating fruit and berries that grew on our property and reading science fiction novels in the trees. Sometime during junior high I started meditating in the woods, though I didn't know to call it that. I would cross the yard, step through the border of Douglas firs, and find some soft, needle-carpeted spot to stare into space and let my mind go empty. Everything I now think about nature and technology rests upon these formative experiences in a zone between what is grown and what was once manufactured, between the wild strength of a sapling and the relentlessness with which rust returns an artifact to the soil.

When my parents sold the property in 1999 in the same month I got married, I grieved. I understood their rationale for moving but lamented their leaving the acreage where so much of my imagination had taken root. By this time I had embraced an urban life in Seattle. In retrospect, my move to a city had always been a foregone conclusion. Around age ten I came upon an illustration in a magazine, of Lewis Carroll's Alice, her body composed of gears and cables, monitors and spools of print-out paper. This captivating image was captioned "Alice in Technology Land." I asked my mother what technology meant, and while I can't remember her response, I do remember thinking it was a profound concept I would need to pay attention to the rest of my life. By the time I was twenty-five I had picked bulbs in tulip fields and managed a customer database in an office park. I'd watched lambs being born and stock prices spike into hundreds of dollars per share. It's the places where what we erroneously call the "natural" and "man-made" worlds commingle where I felt most at home.

When I was an undergraduate ice cream man peddling Fudgsicles in the suburban grid, I fixated on a mathematical object, the hypercube, also known as the tesseract. A hypercube is a four-dimensional object represented as a cube within a cube. These two cubes are in flux. As the inner cube grows, the outer cube contracts, until they trade places. The cube that was once the content becomes the context, and vice versa. I had been fascinated by this figure since a high school math teacher woke me from my usual fifth-period nap by drawing it on the board. During the requisite sophomore phase of Salvador Dali appreciation, I bought a print of the surrealist's *Corpus Hypercubus*, which depicts Christ crucified on the net—or unfolded geometrical extraction—of a hypercube. This image led me to believe that certain human constructs—religion and media in particular—had overpowered the experience of being an individual body in the throes of perception to the point that these constructs, rather than our individual, perceptual selves, were the frames within which we comprehended and measured reality. What was a television set sitting in a house if not one recontextualizing cube within another? When I hear of meteorologists getting stopped in the street and blamed for storms, or of virtual goods in video games being purchased with actual money, or when I read Don DeLillo's prescient *White Noise* in which a family's sense of urgency during an environmental catastrophe is framed as a struggle to comprehend sudden, unmediated reality, then I feel as if the screen has passed through my body and can no longer be contained by my consciousness. Rather, my consciousness operates within the machinery of the representational.

While keeping the hypercube in mind, I was also obsessed with a diagram of three concentric circles I drew in my notebook whenever the ice cream sandwiches ran out. The center circle I labeled "technology." The middle circle I labeled "humanity." And the outer circle I labeled "nature." The content of technology could not exist outside the context of human invention. The content of humanity could not exist outside the context of nature. Hence technology, regardless of whatever destructive properties it might possess, was a natural phenomenon. Our notion of the "artificial" was itself an artificial distinction.

What if we were to combine these models, then? What if this nested model of nature, humanity, and technology were granted the dynamic, recontexualizing properties of a hypercube? Might we then imagine a reality in which humanity encompassed nature within consciousness? Or in which technology became the contextual framework for humanity? This led me to the works of writers like Bill McKibben, Neil Postman, Marshall McLuhan, Sven Birkerts, and Jean Baudrillard.

In the alarmingly titled *The End of Nature*, McKibben compares a day in the woods to a day's worth of cable television, pitting the inanities of infomercials against the sublime pleasure of skinny-dipping beneath the stars. Postman, in the years before the raging hard-on of the World Wide Web, laments the tendency of digital culture to turn us into distracted, agitated, dumbed-down creatures. Baudrillard, whose works inspired the popular *Matrix* franchise, spoke of the negation of the concept of reality, of life that passed through a series of simulations with no originals. McLuhan, the giant in the field of media studies, informed my emerging comprehension of the Internet by suggesting that the content of any new medium is an old medium. And Birkerts, in his book *The Gutenberg Elegies*, defined the battle lines between the literary culture I loved and the digital culture that was exerting a greater pull on my attention. Most of what I attempted to absorb in these and other works went over my head, and I oriented my understanding to what was artistically interesting rather than what struck me as particularly applicable. I kept circling around questions about the White Noise mindfuck of the televised, as office towers where the next decade's technologies percolated rose amid salmon streams and vine maples.

As a kid in the woods I fantasized about what I would do to survive the wake of global nuclear catastrophe and I have been haunted throughout my adulthood by the intertwined threats of climate change, overpopulation, and pollution. I can never remember a time when it hasn't been an article of faith that humanity's technologies are capable of destroying life on earth and that this process is well underway. The suspicion that planet earth is completely, irrevocably fucked and there's nothing we can do about it is a sentiment my generation has become cozy with. It's the comforting pessimism I reached for to protect my heart from sinking completely as I watched streaming footage of oil streaming into the Gulf of Mexico. The we-put-a-man-on-the-moon confidence in technological solutions gets dusted off once again in order to once again be proved misplaced. We find ourselves perplexed that, while our faith in the redemptive potential of our ingenuity remains unshaken, we're impotent against global market capitalism's unyielding demand that we make more things cheaper in order to make fewer and fewer people wealthier. We sense that this is killing us and yet privately we know there's absolutely nothing we can do about it. We're like an insane psychiatrist attempting to devise for himself a cure.

In a sense we're all on some point in a sort of Kubler-Ross continuum when it comes to the death of our species on planet earth. Fringe Christian dominionists scoff in denial at the overwhelming scientific proof the human race is changing the temperature of earth while simultaneously insisting that it is our divine right to do so. I've heard Tea Party rallies chant the word "bullshit" in response to inquiries as to the veracity of climate science. While those on the politically conservative side of arguments about climate change cultivate their scoffs in protective, willful ignorance of a problem too terrifying to confront, those on the left pull the old religious tools of guilt and the assumption that human beings are ultimately sinful as they scold. On the bargaining side of this ideological divide, I've been shamed into using only one napkin at Whole Foods, to which I bring my own bag made of recycled plastic bottles. I've also heeded the admonitions of rock stars who want me to use a different kind of light bulb.

What I'm prepared to argue is that this scoff and scold dichotomy is destructive, and both positions are based on certain assumptions rooted in our inability to think within the contextual framework of a dynamic nature/humanity/technology hypercube.

For the climate change deniers, theirs is a rebellion against their own neocortexes in which their capacity for rationality presumably lies. It is a natural, burrowing reaction that allows these people to not become paralyzed in an increasingly alarming, maddening, confusing civilized world.

Those on the progressive left, who have come to grasp the empirical reality of our changing planet, simply apply the same narrative template of victim vs. antagonist they apply to any number of problems involving groups and classes of human beings. In a fit of anthropomorphizing egotism we've managed to project our own victimhood complexes onto the entire planet. The environmental movement, broadly speaking, has relegated earth to its own category of aggrieved minority, even granting it its own "day." But self-loathing isn't going to return the climate to mellower temperatures. Farley Mowatt, whose *Never Cry Wolf* became a film I watched with some reverence as a child, once said that if he had the chance to press a button and erase human beings from the planet, he would not hesitate to do so. Alan Weisman's fascinating nonfiction book *The World Without Us* imagines what would happen to the planet in this very scenario. How long would our buildings stand? How long would it take before our bridges collapsed and our subways filled with flood water? The subtext of many works of post-apocalyptic speculation is to symbolically punish civilization for its transgressions against this category of reality we call nature. Human selfishness and greed are extrapolated into the most dystopian futures we can envision. But could it be that these compelling warnings fall short in their accusations? Might it be that instead of being too greedy and selfish, we, as a species, are not being greedy and selfish in the right way?

If we can agree that technology exists within the realm of human invention and that humanity exists within natural law, and that therefore technology is natural; if we can dispose of the naturally artificial distinction between "natural" and "artificial," then we can argue that whatever happens to the planet bears no moral value outside that which is relative to our health as a species.

Consider the classic idealized American landscape painting of the Hudson River School of the 19th century, the Albert Bierstadts and Thomas Morans. The vast canyons and meadows touched by shafts of sunlight, the glistening brooks, the abundant foliage and meek little cabins set amid breathtaking Arcadian splendor. What makes such a landscape beautiful? What makes it beautiful is that it looks fit for human habitation. In the art world of flesh eating bacteria, all the paintings depict necrotic human limbs.

I confess to having a rudimentary at best science education, but I profess to be an expert on how to use language, and the language of the progressive environmental movement is hobbled with assumptions. First, we conceive of "the earth" as a place outside the sphere of our daily lives. We speak of "saving the planet" as if the planet is not in our living rooms, our bodies, our cars, our computers and roads. More laughable is the idea that our products can be "earth friendly," one of the most patronizing phrases ever slapped on a roll of toilet paper. The word "sustainability," which has gained currency in recent years represents something between the denial and bargaining stages of the Kubler-Ross process of grieving, applied to a planetary scale. What can "sustainable" mean when the history of our planet involves several eras of mass extinction?

The question isn't whether the planet is changing. The question isn't whether we've caused that change. Those questions have been answered. The real pressing question is why. Not why in the scientific sense, but why in the philosophical sense. To what end are we changing the planet?

Environmental thought can be divided into three broad categories with an emerging fourth—preservationism, restorationism, conservationism, and inventionism. These ways of thinking about our planet with their attendant strategies can overlap, intermingle, and inform one another. Taken as a progression, they can be viewed as stages in a process of defeating the denial, fear, and self-loathing that understandably characterize how we feel about our earth.

The philosophy of environmental preservation, in seeking to keep "unspoiled" nature as it is, draws a distinct line between humanity and nature. Beautiful landscape paintings serve as preservationist pornography, both inviting us to imagine ourselves situated within their frames while disgusting us with the implication that our entry would spoil the "natural" splendor on display. Conservation seeks to manage resources in order that they not be completely depleted. Meanwhile, the restorationist philosophy seeks to restore to its former condition land that has been spoiled by human beings. Examples of successful restorations, such as once-dead lakes that now teem with fish, reward our faith in our own ingenuity and make us feel a little less hopeless that our ecosystem is irreversibly screwed. Restoration ecology ceases to make sense when it presupposes a static state to which a landscape can return. If nature is a system of fluctuations, of an endless negotiation between eros and thanatos, of forest fires caused by lightning, pandemics, and volcanoes paving what once was jungle, then to what "natural" state can a meadow, a river, a mountaintop be restored? Perhaps restorationism's motives are at their most noble when biodiversity, nature's way of hedging its bets, is the ultimate goal.

In the last twenty years or so, a new idea called *inventionism* has flickered on the edges of environmental philosophy, explored in such places as a collection of essays published in 1994 called *Beyond Preservation: Restoring and Inventing Landscapes*. Inventionism suggests that we must graduate from a purely reactive orientation to environmental catastrophes and geo-engineer ourselves a more biologically diverse planet. We must apply the full intellectual breadth and philosophical depth of our nature-made brains and, in effectively managing the environment of planet earth, learn how we might terraform other planets and spread life broadly beyond our star. I happen to believe that we live at the pivot point when civilization, for too long organized by warring religions, is beginning to slowly cast aside those distinctions in order to realize our new purpose, to become stewards of life that will teem elsewhere in our universe long after our shadow has faded.

For now, though, we struggle, confused about the things we call nature, humanity, and technology. Our passivity is our enemy, and the old ignorant scoff and righteous scold paradigm promises the same inertia. If we can begin to think of the earth, the human race, and technology as one, if we can obliterate these old distinctions rooted in dogma and consider that we are the way the earth is figuring out how to keep the seasons coming in their dramas of ice and flowers, then perhaps we can begin to look at the wilderness not as a place from which we've been exiled, but as something that we can compose.

—*Delivered Summer, 2010, Port Townsend, Washington*

INSIDE THE SEISMOGRAPH

by Beatrix Gates

Begun in the waves out from the fall of the Towers/begun in the clearing passages/from behind torn masks. Eyeholes. From behind gaping holes: torn, fired paper shades, blinds torn away, slats cutting both ways. News held in front of the eyes, folded, wadded, cutting off the opening: fire/paper; paper/fire. Eyes wide. Lashes singed, lids stiff. Blinds flipped one way to seal out the sight of willed hurt: bodies hurtled into freefall. Blinds shut to contain the view.

The towers fell straight to the ground, and the fire burned for months, melted steel, a long wick ignited deep into the ground. How could a sky, empty of clouds, be empty? And how could anyone think themselves alone now? Daily news in front of the eyes, a thick pliable shield. Vision no longer a mechanism, but parsed like cloud cover, moving fast, sheer and returning to cloak the orb in darkness, light, to an altered vision of the whole round world.

The explosion/the spray of lives, glass and metal columns spiralling into thickening dust, looking downtown on Amsterdam Avenue into the black envelope of sky (at the tip of Manhattan). Paper—record of our mark, computer printouts, notes, post-its, files—a tide of paper becoming the tide of feet, running, on our streets, paper rising under our feet. Turning tide running high—swells larger than any of the words or their echoes, letters falling into new and altered combinations. New language at our feet, indecipherable.

More paper than shoes, more dust than blackened bones or discernible human wreckage, recognizable organs of life.

An arm, she found an arm, two days in, combing through rubble at the site in the first wave of digging. She was a volunteer who came in at the start, so no one questioned her. She was just there. Every afternoon and into the night picking over the hot clumpy dust next to her boyfriend, the EMT. Bodies melded into a growing, bloodless wordlessness—a silence on the air, in the ground, heard as the burning imprint of breath, all who were here that day in New York City—and the dead with us, under us, in the churning south-borne air.

How to recognize what we didn't see? What haven't we recognized—the words at our feet—and what have we seen? An alphabet of the sky, letters curling in the air. And translation, words cupped to drink from two hands held as one, line on line in the palm, runnels of water, sweat or caking dust. Is this the utterance of our lives, the daily gesture? Hand to mouth. Here and here again—black cloud stays. Blown south, it lives at the bottom of Manhattan, held for days just off the city. A cup of darkness at the lip.

I am walking home, solid smoke billows in the south. Outside Osner's Typewriters & Supplies, there is a dumpster. Three guys, in a running relay, roll a canvas-sided container out to the street. It is filled with heavy typewriters; bulky adding machines with punch keys, round red and white buttons; metal spools for replacement manual typewriter ribbons; thin, shiny tape unwound from typewriter cartridges; heavy black cords and fat connectors. There in the dumpster, the words and every word-maker and number marker of my lifetime from the 40's through the 80's and into the early 90's—the last 50 years—every machine of my lifetime, before the computer, being heaved into a 10 by 20 foot green metal dumpster, overflowing. But there will be no second dumpster. This is it. The end. The keys fallen out, twisted. Most everything sturdier than plastic, much remains whole, dented. Flying ribbons—brown, black, plastic; bunched inked cloth; ribbons on spools like tongues darting between. What language are they whispering in lost torn tongues? The towers sprayed paper out through the shattered glass in the updraft of heat. The dumpster will haul away the useful/used tools of half a century, the contents of the backroom of the typewriter repair shop reduced to scrap. The towers in the first minutes reduced an empire and its holdings to dust. The columns fell as if veined with detonators for a demolition—the surviving trail, a paper flow of dust, dead.

Blinded, seeing, torn away/revealed/blinded by new sight/seeing with partial eyes. Who does the exit belong to? And who creates the entrance to ruin? And what is the shape of meaning of a footprint in the dust, the feel of the imprint, and the response of earth underfoot?

Inside the seismograph: most of September I felt captured, caught inside the seismograph/part of/inside a picture I could not see or read. I could respond like the wavering lines across the page, emotion in ink tracing the impact, waves out—then a steady blank—then the waves out again. It was there in the waves out where I felt I lived and I was not alone—I lived with/I lived with many others. We were together on the sea/together in our buildings, in our streets—we were together as we streamed to the Chelsea Piers on the day after the fall. Coming on foot with shopping carts full of Gatorade and water, car-trunks and back seats stuffed full of sweat pants and socks for firemen and rescue workers continually sodden by water struggling to put out a fire that would not go out and continued burning into late December.

I meet a nurse, an older woman, on the bus, who spoke of leveling, coming to volunteer, sitting on the floor at the Piers, quiet, cross-legged many hours with every kind of doctor, surgeon, therapist, social worker, all sitting on the same floor level waiting to give service, waiting until teams could be made up, waiting for 6, 7, 8, 9, 10 hours. She was gratified to be returning the next day as part of a team.

There was a winding route to deliver clothes and supplies at the piers and the word went out: no more volunteers needed, there are too many. I've been to the Red Cross on the Upper West Side and St. Luke's/Roosevelt where I'm told to return later on. I head downtown by bus to 23rd where I'd heard they needed help. The bus is alive with talk, feels like a vein into New York City, everyone sharing bits of news, stories. At 23rd, I get the word, no more volunteers, but stay and sit and marvel at my city's people. I see a friend, Bell, in a wheelchair with a young friend guiding her chair, both looking for a place to volunteer. She tells me she can do decompression counseling, she's trained, she can listen. She is eager to tell me, someone, anyone what she can offer. We are all ready to do something, anything really. We wait. I tell her I've just heard about St. Luke's needing people in the afternoon. It is good to see each other, a deep flicker of contact. Later, the Piers are set up as a morgue.

Wednesday, September 12th is my second or third week working at the prison and I'm just learning the language "inside." When I enter I pick up my photo ID #95. I am searched with a metal detector and my hand stamped, right or left, with a sign that shows under the black light, last contact before the tunnel of barbed wire beyond the iron gate. My bag is well searched, but it varies, week to week, how thoroughly I am gone over. The gates open on one side: I enter the space, and the gates behind me close. I hold my hand up to the black light where the stamp can be read. I am between two gates, both closed. When the other side opens, I walk through a tunnel of wire fencing surrounded and topped by layers of razor wire. I walk through into the open. To my left is a larger gate, guarded by a tower with armed guards, that can swing open for large vehicles. I face a low flat brick building, like a primary school building and walk the driveway to the path, skirted by flower beds and newly planted cherry trees. Often, there are one or two staff smoking outside, people just getting off work—if I come in between 5 and 6. On the 12th all classes are cancelled at the prison—all visiting —all contact or movement in or out. The prison is locked down—they are in lock.

The prison is locked down during any time of a national security crisis.

On the 12th, NYC is locked down—all bridges, all tunnels. No travel below 14th Street without an ID and proof of residence. A police line cordons off 14th St., both directions, east to west.

The prison can go into lock because of something that happens inside—a violent incident, a search, or because of something outside—a national security crisis, or something we will never know about that falls somewhere in between. Security is secret. Security stays secret. There are no reasons given. There is no negotiation. I may hear pieces of the story later, the next week, the next day, depending on how fresh the news is and whether it stays within the prison walls.

I have been told to bring in no evidence of where I live or work. I have also been told not to ask about any prisoner's time or crime, verbally, or in writing. Any writing I do for publication has to be cleared.

When I tell the women the next week about looking for a place to volunteer, riding the bus around Manhattan, wanting to help and feeling useless and helpless—they tell me that's the way they feel all the time. At the break one of the women approaches me. She gets very close to my face and peers at me as if she could see into my shoes and where my feet have been. She asks: "How is the world?"

I have no big picture. Like many women of North America who are artists and writers of this time, I have changing pictures of a changing life, and I am lucky to have been able to make change, in some small ways. With few impediments, by some standards, I've achieved relative comfort, performing my teaching duties and writing tasks, and answering my calling—poetry that sharpens my days and wakes me day and night. This much I do on a daily basis, like breathing. Most with attention, some worry, not enough lightness, at times.

Living in New York City, I felt the need, with my partner, to commit to domestic partnership and within New York City, we agreed to enter together into a circle of "rights," not offered other places. We did it for fun, and it was serious, in the tradition of many gay and lesbian transactions—deeply serious, because it acknowledged our terms on our own terms; fun and joyous, because we have to keep creating that space of uplift between us or we have nothing, with or without that piece of paper. We keep tight hold of that space in this time, because we know some kinds of danger and threat as daily experience, and maintaining sanity on our own terms in love requires vigilance.

My world is circumscribed and opened by the work I do. The people I work with are a saving grace—the world outside has always been a saving place—a saving grace for me. I have found comfort and safety in the good will of strangers, faith in the sameness of human need, and welcome in many communities—teaching, artists and writers, lgbt folk, women, neighbors, and in being an outsider. Inside, I have found direction often guided by the body, dreams and imagination, not seen as so separate by the lgbt community. Also, inspired by love—and that love includes the work of other artists.

In our first trip out of New York after the fall of the towers, on the weekend after September 11th, we decide to go to an International Puppet Festival and see an amazing and surprising performance by CREO, a Bulgarian puppetry duo performing Gogol's "The Overcoat." The entire performance is inside the coat, and the two puppeteers trace all the prisons of man—social shame and disdain, love and punishment, big crimes and small horrors—displaying the ugly guts of petty competition and small hypocrisies—making us laugh and suck in our breath, open our eyes in wonder. We travel into the true refreshment of imagination and vivid depiction of the cruelties of man. So it is—this world opens through the love and care brought to this production of Gogol's truths. We are ready to receive. CREO imagined inside the world of the coat, skeleton, spine and flesh of this flawed struggling human, and envisioned a show with the love required for the flawed person and for the struggle.

This attention and care is the same kind of love that the writer James Baldwin requires of us when he returns, over and over again, to the necessity of confronting and recognizing all that disrupts us, terrifies us. This we must do to be able to love. Baldwin says that without risk, there cannot be any true giving. And if we cannot look at ourselves, we cannot know what it is to really be equal or to be free, in a deeply spiritual and political sense. He speaks of the two as one—and shows how dream can blur to nightmare without conscious investigation of our lives; our country or our reality. History must be faced, and pride let go, or the American Dream will suffocate us in its own claustrophobia. He exhorts us in *The Fire Next Time* to arrive into reality and bear the burdens of discovering exactly what that is.

Baldwin was accused of not standing firmly enough with his people, not standing for his people, being too Black, straying too far towards Malcolm X, deserting his country, losing his passion, becoming bitter— all by *The New York Times*. But no verbal lynching in the *NYT* can undo the love he proposed, lived, and told through his writing.

If we continue to focus on the triumph and uncertainty of the individual without renewing ourselves or allowing failure to teach us, then we will be trapped by the seduction of a preference for ease, for heaven, for vacation, for all that says, 'It' is good and perfect in our lives; and better than 'you' and your poverty and your dirty children and your illiteracy, and your speaking three or four languages, when clearly, there is only one—one language, one God. This is a problem. Where then is the entrance to ruin? And where is the exit? What language(s) will we speak when we cross over?

Where are we? And who is we? In the first cold blood that flushed my veins seeing the Towers fall, I thought with fear: What are they going to do now? This president, selected, not elected, in what amounts to a coup, would have no limits on his authority.

I found myself standing wordless, intentionally silent, on the street, with a cadre of a hundred others at Times Square, with the words: "Do not turn our grief into a cry for war," stenciled on a T-shirt on my back, highlighted in black and white. With many signs, we turned out toward the traffic and movement of the street. I stood in horror in Times Square as a new Christian Crusade of unmitigated arrogance and cruelty seemed to be literally racing overhead and all around us at unimaginable speeds. So how can we enter and re-enter this world? Even if we have health, food, and shelter, we need communion, a real desire to connect; and to experience love and loving others. Baldwin is one of the few to offer— cogently, painfully—clear terms, rare in their brilliance, for taking responsibility, and he names the price of avoidance and continued arrogance. We must learn to answer his call, somehow.

Perhaps we can learn to love not only by looking at ourselves in our own light, but by looking at ourselves from other times and other places. What time is it in Kabul? What are you wearing, and have you eaten when you hear the sound of the planes? Enemy planes? Friendly planes? Policing helicopters? Who is being policed and by whom exactly? Can you see your hand in the dark? Do you have a match? Do you have electricity? For how many hours a day? At night? A lantern? Water? Is the water sweet? Or is the water poisoned, and how did that happen?

Inside the seismograph, each day a different strata revealed—the relationship of all things turning, by the hour, the minute—time turned, pulled. The plates of stone under Manhattan squeezed, earth to gravel crushed, rotating columns of fire deep into the earth, stone heating stone, taking it all in. The granite took it in. The buildings stood—we who remained, remained unreadable—flesh changed and still unable to read ourselves outside of the shock of our collective grief. For two weeks after 9/11, I couldn't read a thing—the experience of time did not allow for the digestion of outside reading. I only had an appetite for direct, personal contact, steady, good music and hourly information from the jazz station, WBGO. Voices of friends reconnecting right afterwards, no sleep against the blankness and waving sea—and a need for more contact after the first bone-deep, blood-cold wash of fear, wash of horror. What will they do? And then how will they stop?

There could be no reading at the site of impact, just the power of change, but there was no measure, no division of realities, only the impact of change flowing outward from change flowing outward, these waves and their measure could be called power.

To enter the picture at all means giving. I had my body, midlife, I had the ability to hear and to observe—I had speech, one language, another I could read and speak quite well, a third I am learning and love, one I hated in school upon which all three could stand as different bridges over changing waters, contiguous and divergent. I must learn to love what I hated. Needing all my faculties, I feel the x-ray of all my frailties, wish for my grandmother's fluency in numerous languages, and all that touched her like the many-tongued river she must have dreamt in at night. When I did read in the month of September, only poetry spoke to me.

I was scheduled to give a reading with the poet Marilyn Hacker in Ram Deveni's series at the St. Agnes Branch of the NYPL on Saturday, September 15th, 3 blocks from where I live. I have never felt so in need of a poetry reading, or so deeply privileged to be giving a poetry reading. There was a space offered and I could bring something to it. I had my poems, and I had somewhere to go. I looked through folders, spread the typed and scrawled across the floor and futon, pulled out my book *In the Open*, and books of others.

I looked through Muriel Rukeyser's *Poem to Kathe Kollwitz* where she offers: "... I am in the world/to change the world." Followed by: "... and death holding my lifetime between great hands/the hands of enduring life/that suffers." Rukeyser names the wide dilemma and holds it out to us, embodied.

In Carolyn Forché's collection, *The Angel of History*, meeting life's consequences, for an artist, has to be a daily experience. "Surely all art is the result of one's having been in danger, of having gone through an experience all the way to the end." Our September, and all that is to come, a live echo in her words.

And the French poet, Paul Éluard, extended the grief implicit in Rukeyser and Forché, and states his anger in *Seven Poems of Love in*

War, 1943: "Shame of unbounded evil/Shame of our absurd butchers/ Always the same always." And later in the poem, Eluard joins all peoples caught in war, when he says, "But we are not ashamed of our suffering/ We are not ashamed of our shame/Not even a bird is left alive." Eluard stands for facing destruction and staying human in the face of it.

When we spoke, Marilyn Hacker and I agreed that we should read poets from other parts of the world, as a sign of the connectedness of us all. So she brought her translations of Claire Malroux's poems about daily surviving Naziism, WWII France. And she read W.H. Auden's *1939* to our gathering at the library branch, "All I have is a voice/To undo the folded lie..." and the famous, "We must love one another or die." The homeless people sat in the front row and slept—their shelter had stayed the same, the library held them safe. We read together, and then gathered afterwards in the living room of my apartment at West 79th Street. We spoke few words, but moved in and out of small clusters. There was a palpable feel of the need to gather. The poems did their work, we shared food and drink, and we spoke together softly.

The language had changed—all the words sounded different, the space between them changed, the weight altered, mysterious subjects suddenly stark; electric metaphors turned to dust. The pattern of circulation and life in the poems entirely different. I follow these veiny roots and branches with surprise and anticipation and begin to find a new path where life blood begins to flow more freely. Across the earth, the words defining and creating a relation to all the sources.

—*Delivered Winter, 2002, Plainfield, Vermont*

BEAST, BEAUTY, BELOVED
By Aimee Liu

> *"Accursed creator! Why did you form a monster so hideous that even you turned from me in disgust? God, in pity, made man beautiful and alluring, after his own image; but my form is a filthy type of yours, more horrid even from the very resemblance."*

Thus spake Dr. Frankenstein's MFA thesis project. Created in a fever of noble ambition, with the prospective graduate's entire academic community waiting in breathless anticipation...and still the final product is nowhere near perfect! Whose fault is it, anyway? Surely not the monster's itself.

No, it's always about the creator.

A curse indeed! What hubris, what arrogance, what madness it is to think that we mere mortals can create a work of art that would do justice to the human condition. We strive for beauty and, of course, like Mary Shelley's genius Frankenstein, we produce instead a beast.

Worse, even as this curse of creativity promises glory, it turns us into beasts ourselves. Poor Dr. Frankenstein narrates a tale that every graduating student knows only too well:

> The leaves of that year had withered before my work drew to a close; and now everyday showed me more plainly how well I had succeeded. But my enthusiasm was checked by my anxiety, and I appeared rather like one doomed by slavery to toil in the mines, or any other unwholesome trade than an artist occupied by his favorite employment. ...I grew alarmed at the wreck I perceived that I had become; the energy of my purpose alone sustained me: my labors soon would end, and I believed that exercise and amusement would then drive away incipient disease; and I promised myself both when my creation should be complete.

Alas, no commencement, not matter how lavish, elegant, or brimming with praise, can free creator from creature. Again poor Frankenstein knew this well:

> ...now that I had finished, the beauty of the dream vanished, and breathless horror and disgust filled my heart.

His creation was finished but not complete! Revision yet awaited. Revision and, dare I say, understanding?

> I felt what the duties of a creator towards this creature were, and that I ought to render him happy before I complained of his wickedness.

But how to achieve such a rendering? How can we possibly make happy a beast that emerges from such misery as the creative process? What will it take to satisfy something so monstrous, so insatiable, so unfathomable?

I suggest we begin with simple respect. The creature only wants what we all want: to be known, to be seen and heard to the depths of its being, to be judged not by its superficial flourishes or obvious excesses, but by its heart—its core, abiding truth. To bring its deepest subject matter up to the surface in a way that doesn't make its creator turn away in shame.

Frankenstein's creature said as much when he told his creator:

> "Once my fancy was soothed with dreams of virtue, of fame, and of enjoyment. Once I falsely hoped to meet with beings who, pardoning my outward form, would love me for the excellent qualities which I was capable of unfolding. I was nourished with high thoughts of honour and devotion."

Oh, but that outward form can be insurmountable! People will judge a book by its cover! Readers will judge a creature not just by the content of its characters but also by the shapeliness of its prose. Not all creatures can be beauties—or Oprah picks. Some are born to be beasts, like Frankenstein's, "degraded beneath the meanest animal."

So what's a creator to do?

Press on, is my advice. Dig deeper into your creature's soul. What does it mean for this being to live and breathe and speak? Who is it? What is it? Where did it come from? What is the point—the purpose—of its creation? Search these questions and honor them, for as Frankenstein's monster pleaded with his maker:

> "I cannot believe that I am the same creature whose thoughts were once filled with sublime and transcendent visions of the

beauty and majesty of goodness. But it is even so; the fallen angel becomes a malignant devil."

As creators we are forever bound to the creatures we create, angels and devils alike. They define us even as we define them. We owe them our lives even as they depend on ours for theirs. We become them as they become us. Love them, or loathe them, as artists we cannot live without them.

But if we know what is good for the creative process, we will follow Mary Shelley's lead and allow, nay, exploit, the fact that no one can either love or loathe the product of his creation. Inherent in the creative process is a perpetual tension between love and loathing that gives art its life. As writers we are naturally torn between controlling our story and letting it fly, between resisting our characters and surrendering to them, between delighting in our creation and despising it. Shall we kill the Beast? Truncheon it into submission? Or embrace it, even down to its last dangling participle? We must do all; we can do none. The act of creation is innately paradoxical. We can never wholly possess what we produce, but we can never wholly let it go.

Understand this paradox, respect and be mindful of it, and, yes, love it, too. If you do, the tension will become a source of power in your creative process, rather than your downfall. Your creatures deserve your love and compassion—even though, and also because, they are extensions of you.

Persevere! No matter how ugly, how deformed, how horrid a mirror your monster may seem, give it all the passion you possess. And when—and only when—you have no more to give, then take Mary Shelley's sage advice and, with great tenderness and hope, bid your hideous progeny, "Go forth and prosper."

—*Delivered Summer, 2008, Port Townsend, Washington*

SOURCE
Mary Shelley, *Frankenstein.* Ed. Maurice Hindle. New York: Penguin Books, 1992.

III. Aesthetic Ambition

READING AT THE BOTTOM OF THE WORLD
By Victoria Nelson

Recently a cultivated woman expressed dissatisfaction to me about the last few books her reading group had selected. They had been diligent in choosing only those new novels enthusiastically endorsed by *The New York Times* and other reviewing organs, discussed on National Public Radio, and blurbed by famous writers. Yet the works in question disappointed; expectations had not been fulfilled. How could this be?

There are many ways to answer this question, but I want to respond from the way it looks from the Bottom of the World—that is, from the Bolinas perspective.

Bolinas, California, is a tiny coastal village just north of the Golden Gate Bridge with a still-flourishing tradition of flouting controlled substance laws that dates back to Prohibition days, when bootleggers smuggled in whiskey by high-speed launch. Flanked by a silted-in lagoon where sea lions lounge under the rolling bosom of Mount Tamalpais, boasting a clear view straight down the coast, on fogless days, of the gleaming white city of San Francisco, Bolinas still enjoys a reputation as an iconoclastic bohemian enclave even as increasing numbers of well-heeled folk driving late-model off-road vehicles cruise its Wharf Road, a two-block row of Victorian wooden storefronts.

I think of Bolinas as the Bottom of the World, in a good sense. Geographically it's about as far west as you can get in the continental United States without falling into the ocean. Culturally it's distinctly, self-consciously separate from American mainstream intellectual culture. Standing on the cliffs looking out at the wet-suited surfers on chilly Duxbury Reef, walking the misty trails of the Point Reyes seashore that start on Bolinas Mesa, I feel I am occupying a place apart that still belongs, that gives me the best and truest perspective on the larger economic and cultural megasociety that North Americans and Europeans share. And most particularly it gives me a priceless outsider's perspective on what is closest to my heart: books and literary culture. (I can never forget both the shock and the acute cultural disjuncture I felt some years ago reading Richard Brautigan's obituary, datelined Bolinas, in the *London Times*.)

The view from the Bottom of the World, put briefly, rejects the impulse to heed the voice of authority favoring instead an egalitarian, open-minded curiosity. Applied to books, it offers a way out of a dilemma experienced by intelligent people who look to the media for guidance in their reading. From the Bolinas perspective, I would answer the woman from the book club like this: Why would you ever want to believe what the concentrated forces of consensus and marketing tell you about any product that requires you to take your wallet out of your pocket?

Far in advance of publication, a book's fate—and particularly the fate of that most perishable of commodities, a novel—has already been sealed by an elaborate process of status positioning: which agent represented it to which editor at what level of which publishing house; the book's placement, high or low, on the house's season list; the marketing and promotion budget assigned to it; and the level of word-of-mouth interest it has aroused in the very small centralized world of New York publishing. This elaborate prepublication ranking is communicated by publishers' sales representatives and press releases to booksellers and reviewing organs national and regional, determining which precious few in the Noah's flood of books published every year will bob to the surface—that is, be both reviewed and physically present in stores (and, via the ubiquitous practice of "cooperative" funding from the publisher, given preferential display). As a rule, the new books that educated Americans "hear about" via reviews, advertising, and talk shows represent only that tiny percentage about which uniformly favorable business decisions have been made long before their pages were even typeset.

Authors and book-business people are keenly aware of, and attuned to, this draconian screening process. Because it is invisible to them, most readers are not. When they see multiple reviews and mentions of a new novel, they believe it has received this attention out of simple merit. They do not hear, rising off the newspaper or magazine page, the ghostly clamor of the scores of equally meritorious novels published at the same time that did not receive this, or any other, review—or the even fainter cries of the legion of worthy books never published at all.

(My Borgesian fantasy: if all the unpublished books in the world switched places with all the published books, what kind of a literature would we possess? Might we in fact inhabit a literary universe very similar to the present one, featuring a continuum of wonderful, good, and less good works?)

Enter the Bolinas Friends of the Library booksale, held at the Bolinas Community Center on Wharf Road, where the flotsam of First World publishing resurfaces in all its unscreened glory. These modest quarters (also the venue of the AfroCuban fusion aerobics class on Sunday mornings) offer the truly independent reader the rare opportunity to discover her only pure road to taste, what I like to call the Naked Encounter between reader and text. The Naked Encounter is something like what the old New Criticism was after, only a bit more stripped down and accessible to all. When the only "buzz" rising off the pages of these old hardbacks lined up in rows on cafeteria tables is the familiar stink of foggy coastal mildew, the selection criteria become severely narrowed. Faced with ancient hardbacks that have long since shed their jackets, absent the "staff picks" and "hand-sold" mythos of the independent booksellers (as if these good people were themselves magically isolated and exempt from sales reps' pitches and the barrage of publishers' promotional materials), minus the clever paragraph summaries in the catalogs of lost masterpieces offered by remainder outlets, sans critical signposts of any kind, you are truly on your own. There is only the Naked Encounter between you and a book, with no guidelines whatsoever save gut instinct. And this random unmediated encounter is the single most essential ingredient in developing taste.

Over the years I have culled many books, awful and wonderful, from the Bolinas semiannual event: Balzac's novel *Séraphita*, an incoherent mishmash of undigested Swedenborgian philosophy that clearly show the results of too much caffeine on the author's nervous system (he drank fifty cups a day, a fact the adulatory preface fails to mention). *Séraphita* in its day, the year 1834, was a great success, and so, I imagine, was the American proletarian novel published a century later and also offered for sale in Bolinas. Written entirely in Okie pidgin and dedicated to the author's muse, "Miss Emma Stein of the WPA," this book displays a sheer impenetrability that speaks volumes about the ways in which topical issues, the floating cultural Zeitgeist of any given time, act to cloud our perceptions of literary worth. Novels we read because they show us lives we have never seen before fulfill an important purpose, but we don't realize, until the necessary decades have passed, how many of these earnest works date as relentlessly as the shallowest bodice ripper. At the Bolinas sale I found also a well-written, beautifully constructed novel by Edna Ferber—the Danielle Steel of her day, we might say—that triggered some thoughts about just how far the standards of popular genre novels have sunk.

I had as well the great pleasure of buying, in the little used clothing/junk store around the corner from the Bolinas Community Center, a first edition hardcover copy of a quintessential Bolinas novel: Louis B. Jones's *California's Over*. Set in the late 1970s, it's the sad-hilarious tale of moving day for the survivors of an ultra-hip Bolinas family whose paterfamilias (possibly sketched after Brautigan himself) committed suicide. Sentence for sentence (I might have some small quibbles about the narrative structure), this book is a world-class reading experience. Why Louis B. Jones is not as well known as some other current literary fiction writers who are his distinct inferiors is an important question, and one that can only come from the Bottom of the World.

Of course, neither the Bolinas Friends of the Library Sale nor the town junk store is free of marketing influences and cultural weighting, predetermined in this case by a complex local cultural stratigraphy of educated summer folk from the very old days overlaid by hippies and New Agers from the more recent old days. (You are much more likely, for example, to find Elizabeth Claire Prophet's *Cosmic Consciousness* offered here than in other town library sales.) And all library sales feature disproportionate numbers of the chunky hardcover bestsellers they are forced to overbuy every year to keep up with a reader demand that is almost entirely generated by market hype. (A rogue element of random selection, it must be noted, has always infected that quintessentially American shrine of prescreening aesthetics, the Book of the Month Club, thanks to the fact that the bookshelves of its members have traditionally been filled with unwanted volumes they forgot to send in the chit for saying they didn't want. This fine-print loophole, which succeeded in generating a goodly portion of the book club's revenue in its heyday, created countless home libraries based almost entirely on negative selection.)

After the library or church sale the next best venue of randomness is a truly chaotic used bookstore, always to be favored over the better-run establishments. Readily identified by the stacks of unsorted books that clog the aisles, such a store emits a general air of melancholia that is usually symptomatic of a mild personality disorder in its owner but offers a gold mine for a reader at any stage of taste development. Untainted by the presence of anything remotely resembling a critical selection process, these pack-rat establishments are just about the closest thing to a retail book flea market you can find. They are a perfect setting for the Naked Encounter.

Now it might be argued that the used bookstore's even more laissez-faire Internet progeny—Amazon.com, eBay, Advanced Book Exchange, and other cyberspace clearinghouses for every book ever published—represent the quintessence of randomness. The Naked Encounter, however, is next to impossible online, for the simple reason that, even though you use a "browser," you can't browse. There are lists and subject categories and so on, but nothing that allows you to pick up the book in question and look at it. (First chapter offerings from *The New York Times* online and its affiliate Barnes & Noble don't count; they are elite marketing tools for a handful of prescreened books.)

After used bookstores proper comes the marketing level known in the *Village Voice*'s felicitous phrase as Remainderama. Remaindered book outlets are based on sheer Darwinian supply and demand principles that decree the scuttling of books after a very short lifetime on the shelves. While bookstores devoted solely to remaindered books do have a desirable wild card air about them, mail-order establishments such as Daedalus deal exclusively in staff-screened and intelligently blurbed remaindered books. A quiet pond compared to that Sargasso Sea of endless possibility that a library sale offers—and thus not as efficacious in developing taste—but still a vast improvement over self-enslavement to a this-season "new and notable" reading creed. For a mere $4.95 plus postage and handling I obtained from Daedalus a copy of Thomas Bernhard's novella *Gargoyles*, a fine reading experience during which my occasional lapse in attention was more than compensated for by an abiding admiration for the story's general outrageousness (it culminates in a fifty-page monologue delivered by a schizophrenic aristocrat).

Long before I ever came across places like Bolinas, Remainderama was the locus of my own early literary education. In my childhood my family lived on a boat in Florida, far from bookstores of any kind, an experience that imprinted me permanently with the sense that books were not a commodity one could purchase, new, in a shop. (The family cat was named Marlboro after Daedalus's distinguished mail-order predecessor.) Never able or willing, for most of my life, to plunk down full price for a brand new book, I culled used bookstores, returned my used books for more used books, and only on special occasions allowed myself the slightly more costly treat of a remainder. Such a present to myself was M.H. Abrams' *Natural Supernatural*, which I came upon shortly after it had been beached and left for the hermit crabs by advancing waves of literary theory. Reading books at this delicate juncture in their lives, at the moment they cease to be the cutting edge but are not quite passé, is about the most valuable literary education a person can have. A reader coming fresh to such a book is granted a Proustian experience that imparts a whole way of thinking scented with the bittersweet odor of nostalgia already rising off the page.

The single most important lesson in taste a person can receive in any of these venues, however, is this: What's hot now will soon not be. Because of constantly shifting fashion that often looks, from the Bolinas perspective, to be the result of some kind of collective hypnosis, novels seem most susceptible to this effect. Code words clearly signaling mass delusion, in reviews and advertising alike, are "luminous," "seamless," "life altering"—the list goes on and on. (There's nothing the least bit luminous or seamless about *Gargoyles*, I'm happy to report.) To allow the smoke to dissipate, full critical clarity requires the passage of years, many years. Pick up a celebrated work from, say, the 1950s and you discover that the fulsome reviews and testimonials, the gold star of book prizes emblazoned on the cover, all the accoutrements Dame Fama and excellent market positioning can bestow have faded in a manner quite satisfying to the sensibility of an ex-medievalist like me. James Gould Cozzens's *By Love Possessed*—what a highbrow hot ticket that book was when it came out! My mother even had a new hardbound copy; I believe it was a gift from her best friend, her sister-in-law Lucile, who lived in the Boston area and was quite a bit more courant than my family, anchored as we were on the Choctawhatchee Bay in the Florida panhandle, fifty miles from the Okefenokee Swamp. Who today reads or has even heard of James Gould Cozzens, the John Updike of his time? Time to locate a copy and find out, at last, if it's any good. Last month I bought Jonathan Franzen's *The Corrections* for a dollar at a church sale. It's too soon, but we shall see.

Cultivated over time, the plunge into randomness grants on a regular basis the near-miracles that come from a deeply intuitive, inner-guided relationship to books. You find that treasures seeking the right home will fly into your hands. Some years ago, in a bookshop in Hay-on-Wye, the famous English used bookstore town that is now the site of a literary festival, such a book popped out of the shelf at me: a vintage 1916 novel with the title *Pincher Martin O.D.* ("A Story of the Inner Life of the Royal Navy"), whose author bore the salty nom de plume "Taffrail." It's safe to say this jingoistic tale of a lovable Cockney seaman during World War I has no redeeming literary merit on its own, but what of William Golding's great novel of the same name, about a hapless sailor blown off a naval ship during World War II and beached on a mysteriously disintegrating island that proves to be his own shrinking consciousness in the face of death?

This second *Pincher Martin* had been a talisman of my adolescent reading, and my love for its author endured and deepened in later years. So I ventured to write Golding about my find, inquiring after his ironic intentions regarding it—for surely he had provided, with a vengeance, his own superior version of an "inner life of the Royal Navy"? I received, in rapid succession, two postcards, each containing a hand-written note scrawled around a beautifully typeset statement declaring that "William Golding regrets that he cannot answer questions about his books. If he did so he would have no time for anything else." The first stated:

> Thank you for your letter. *Pincher Martin O.D.* would have been O.D. stands for Ordinary Deckhand, a cut below A.B. (Able Bodied Seaman.) I had forgotten "Taffrail's" book when I wrote mine. "Pincher" means "to steal." It is the navy nickname for anyone called Martin but I don't know why.—WG

A week later, with no explanation, the second card arrived:

> *Pincher Martin O.D.* will have been quite well-known, as the Royal Navy has tended to be idolised in Great Britain. I fail to make "ironical historical comments" myself, though my readers seem to find them. However, I'm glad you have found pleasure in my work.

My high opinion of Golding, incidentally, is not shared by the Anglo-American literary establishment, which seems collectively to have judged his later magnificent trilogy—*Rites of Passage, Close Quarters. Fire Down Below*—to be little more than a set of jaunty old-fashioned sea stories in the spirit of Horatio Hornblower or the Patrick O'Brian series.

This discrepancy in critical judgment brings me again to the question of cultural intermediaries. The greater name recognition of personages delivering an opinion in print should never blind a reader to their fallibility and, more important, to their proximity and hence vulnerability to the hype that selected new books receive—a hype that exerts tremendous pressure on them (and on descending tiers of newspaper book reviewers and booksellers in turn) to focus on these works at the expense of more quietly published works. The Bottom of the World is a state of mind that lets you decide for yourself what is good and what isn't without the tiresome interruption of corrupt-without-really-meaning-to-be pundits.

In the all-important process of deciding to buy a book and read it, then, I want to tell my friend and her book club: Try comparing perspectives with some of these worthies after reading the work in question, not before. Pretend—this is hard to do but worth it—pretend that you have in your hand a jacketless flea market relic. Or, more easily, that everyone quoted on the cover, including the one who wrote the jacket copy, is a liar. Dip into the book itself, not its testimonials. Look at the sentences, the way they fit together. If it's a novel, read the dialogue. Look at the last paragraph, a place where few writers can resist the temptation to emote and inflate—the "Tiepolo effect," a friend of mine once dubbed it.

If you do this—give yourself up to Naked Encounters with the books you select to read, become a critic of one for an audience of one—then your reading experiences, good and bad, will rise to a level of wonder, excitement, and richness that is granted only to the person who learns to seek out the unheralded and depend on her own judgment. Take the trouble to look for books outside "top ten" lists of any kind (bestseller or critical), exert your own taste instead of following others' pronouncements, and let a few years go by before you read what everybody is talking about today. On this path you will rarely go wrong: that is my Bolinas promise.

—*Delivered Winter, 2009, Port Townsend, Washington*
*First published in Raritan Winter, 2004

FAILURE: AN APPRECIATION

by Rebecca Brown

The third track on The Flaming Lips' great *At War with the Mystics*, is a song called "The Sound of Failure/It's Dark...is it Always this Dark?" There's a line that goes: "failure calls her name." I often need to remind myself that I need to hear failure out because by failing at doing an easy thing, a group-think thing, a thing one has been taught to do for one's career, one might be encouraged to make or do or be something more original and true. Because failing as an artist is a necessary thing, a thing I wish I could more easily accept.

There's a short story called *The Fiddler* that tells the tale, in the first person, of a poet whose work has just been rejected by the publisher he sent it to. Here's how it begins:

So my poem is damned, and immortal fame is not for me! I am nobody forever and ever. Intolerable fate!

Snatching my hat, I dashed down the criticism, and rushed out into Broadway, where enthusiastic throngs were crowding to a circus in a side-street near by, very recently started, and famous for a capital clown.

As the story goes on, our writer narrator meets a friend, Standard, and then a friend of this friend, Hautboy, at the circus. Hautboy strikes our writer/narrator as being sincere, of having good humor and a kind and honest heart. Our narrator is attracted by the happiness of Hautboy, whom he describes as having "a sort of divine and immortal air like... some forever youthful god..."

Our narrator asks his friend Standard about Hautboy and learns that Hautboy is "an extraordinary genius" who used to be a world renowned violinist. Hautboy used to be in demand at all the great concert houses. He was "crammed...with fame," gold was showered upon him. However, because his fans kept demanding the same "hits" over and over and over, and Hautboy therefore began to lose his love of playing the violin, he gave up his career—and the accolades and money that went with it. He wanted to be able to play what and when and for whom he wanted. To enjoy, in other words, the pleasures of obscurity, of failure.

"With genius, but without fame he is happier than a king," Standard tells our narrator.

At the end of the story, Standard says to our writer/narrator: "I have heard your poem was not very handsomely received." To which our narrator replies: "Not a word of that, for heaven's sake!" Because he has decided to abandon his dream of artistic fame and learn instead, to play the fiddle.

The Fiddler, written in 1853, was one of a number of works dealing with the theme of "failure"—which included *The Happy Failure* and *Bartleby the Scrivener*—written by Herman Melville after the disastrous reception of his novel *Moby Dick*.

When it was first published in 1851, *Moby Dick* was, in terms of commercial and critical reception, a terrible failure. It was big, sprawling, philosophical, Biblical, encyclopedic, and weird. It was, that is to say, not at all like the earlier "successful" novels Melville had written. Melville's first novel, *Typee*, a fictionalized account of his real life adventures in Polynesia (naked ladies! Cannibals!), was a hit in both the USA and Britain, and his publishers and readers were thrilled when he brought forth a sequel, *Omoo*.

Now, I am not at all dissing popular fiction. I love some of it. What I am dissing is the fact that some writers are punished when they try to expand their repertoire to include other things besides what's popular. When Melville deviated from the kind of popular adventure he'd once written, critics called his work "trash," said it was "muddy foul, and corrupt." One newspaper headline even blared: "HERMAN MELVILLE CRAZY," and members of Melville's family arranged for a consult with a doctor about his sanity.

But Herman Melville had not gone insane. He had simply needed to write outside the standard "formula for success." In a letter to his father-in-law Lemuel Shaw, written while he was composing *Moby Dick*, Melville said about his earlier adventure books:

They are...jobs which I have done for money—being forced to it as other men are to sawing wood... my only desire for their "success" (as it is called) springs from my pocket and not from my heart. So far as I am individually concerned & independent of my pocket, it is my earnest desire to write the sort of books which are destined to "fail"—pardon this egotism.

Around this time, Melville met Nathaniel Hawthorne, whose *Mosses from an Old Manse* the 15-years-younger writer much admired. With Hawthorne, Melville was able to discuss his frustration with the difference between writing for marketplace "success" and writing for and from his soul and mind and heart: "What I feel most moved to write, that is banned—it will not pay. Yet altogether, write the OTHER way, I cannot. So the product is a final hash, and all my books are botches..."

The hash, the botch, that Melville was working on at the time he wrote this letter, was *Moby Dick*. He dedicated it to Hawthorne.

Hawthorne recognized the merits of *Moby Dick* and so did a few other readers. But it was not until the 1920s, seven decades after it was published and three decades after Melville died, that *Moby Dick* was "rediscovered" and began to be regarded as the masterpiece it is.

I wish that every time I was rejected by some arts granting organizations or magazine or publisher I could remember stories like the story of *Moby Dick*. Or the story Upper Skagit elder Vi Hilbert told that was recounted in SAM's 2009 exhibit, S'abadeb—The Gifts: Pacific Coast Salish Art and Artists:

A long, long time ago, there was a clumsy girl so ashamed of her uselessness she ran away to the woods. Through her tears she heard a voice telling her to gather plants and roots in order to fashion a container. The girl gathered the materials and wove them together into a loose basket, which the voice told her to take to the river and dip in to see if it was waterproof. The girl dipped it in and the water ran through, and she heard the voice say, "Try again." So the girl gathered her materials again and made another basket and took it to the river again and again the basket could not hold water. Long story short: The girl had to make the basket four times before it was right, and when she finally did, the voice said, "Good. Nice basket. Now go give it to the oldest woman in your village." The girl, who was almost a woman now, her invention of the art of basket-making having taken that long, was upset. She had done all this work, she had spent all this time to make this thing—and now she was supposed to give it away? "Yes," the voice told her. So the girl, who would soon became a woman, did so, and that is how the First Cedar Basket was made.

Or the story about Park Young Sook, Korea's foremost ceramic artist, who was asked to make a group of moon jars for show in a gallery. A moon jar is a traditional Korean vessel made of two thrown pots, pressed together at their lips to make one. Moon jars developed in the neo-Confucian culture of the Choson era between the 15th and early 20th centuries and are the epitome of Choson sensibility, representing elegance, humility, integrity, purity, and self-control. They are solid white. Traditionally, moon jars have been relatively small—the size you can hold in one or both of your hands. But when Park Young Sook went to look at the gallery and saw how huge it was, she realized that traditionally sized moon jars—which had been made for more intimate settings—would not be right there. So she decided to make really big ones. Although she had been a ceramist for decades, it took Young Sook five years to make a Moon Jar the size she wanted.

It was one of these five-years-in-the-making moon jars that I saw at the Seattle Asian Art Museum a while back, and it was stunning. Even if you didn't know what went into making it, you'd find it just plain beautiful. But when I saw the making-of video, I was just blown away.

In one scene, a bunch of guys are loading some big, white, beautiful pots onto the back of a cart. As I watched the video I thought, they're being kind of cavalier—just popping those babies into the cart like that, with just little pieces of cloth between them. The guys pushed the cart a little way down a path and unloaded the cart, yanking the pots off and hauling them up into these woods. Then I saw the artist, Park Young Sook, standing next to a big shallow hole in the ground. The guys brought the pots over to her and she took a hammer and slammed it right into a pot. The pot broke and she hammered it again and again, into smaller pieces, then kicked the busted pieces of pot into the hole and the guys brought another pot and she did it again. Smashing all these huge big beautiful pots to smithereens.

It turns out that each of those pots had some little flaw or crack or blemish, something most people wouldn't see, but not exactly what the artist wanted. So she knocked apart each "draft" to see how and where it broke apart, then took that knowledge back to her studio and started another pot again. She did this for years, failing and breaking, failing and learning and failing again on the way to make the object she desired.

What am I trying to tell myself?

That artistic "success" doesn't come at once. That you may have to keep trying and trying to create the thing you have envisioned. That even if you make a thing you are proud of, "they" might not like it or get it, or might think that because you have been doing this work for years you are getting paid decently for it, even though you aren't.

That you might need to break a lot of pots, and write a lot of drafts, and that not everyone is going to like what you do. Which is why, however your work is received by "them," you need a good, true, decent friend or two—a friend or family member like Melville had, a writer pal or a bunch of fellow potters, or actual practitioners of art—to believe in you and to understand and bear with you throughout the long hard work of creating your art, of trying to live a life of making art.

Even if you do make something you are proud of, others may not recognize it at the time, if they ever recognize it at all. And if you ever do "succeed" in making art you believe in, you need to be able to give it away.

The sound of failure calls my name.

I'm still trying to learn to live with that. To hear it out and follow it, to fail, as Samuel Beckett said, then fail better. To fail, then fail better, then fail and fail more, but not to stop.

—*A version of this essay was delivered Winter, 2002, Plainfield, Vermont*

WHAT WE TALK ABOUT WHEN WE TALK ABOUT 'AESTHETIC AMBITION'

By Neil Landau

If you're like me, you don't write nearly as much as you could or should, because your career drive just had a head-on collision with your aesthetic ambition.

Or maybe it was your grandiose, idealistic dreams careening out of control and smashing into your midlife crisis—which was parked at the intersection of Denial that you haven't reached your potential yet, and Refusal to Believe that you'll never win an Oscar (or Emmy or Tony).

If you're like me, you've still got plenty of fight in you, but you're tired and bruised by rejection and uncertainty.

If you're like me, you always second-guess yourself, wondering if what you're pouring all of your creative energies into will ever pan out or alchemize into a vein of gold.

If you're like me, you work in a town where "success" is defined monetarily and graded hierarchally, A-list being top dog, C-list and below being considered has-been, never-will-be, or on the ropes, not quite down-for-the-count, but punch drunk and teetering.

I'll be honest with you: my aesthetic and my ambition have been at war with each other since kindergarten. When I'd finger-paint, I didn't just want to make a pretty picture. I wanted my teacher, Mrs. Berg (who had an unfortunate flatulence disorder), to like my picture better than anyone else's in the class. My color palette, my inventive use of positive and negative space, my bold expressionism. I yearned for one of those gold stars she gave out for outstanding achievement.

If comedy is tragedy plus time, in my life tragedy has equaled under-graduate college graduation plus time. I graduated from UCLA Film School with a Screenwriting emphasis in 1985. My best friend there was, and to a large degree, still is, A-list screenwriter David Koepp.

If that name doesn't ring a bell for you, then I'm sure that the title of at least one of the blockbusters he's written over the past fifteen years will. Among them, please, take your pick:

Jurassic Park
Jurassic Park 2

Mission Impossible
Panic Room
War of the Worlds
Indiana Jones and the Crystal Skull
Snakes Eyes
Secret Window
Death Becomes Her
The forthcoming prequel to *The DaVinci Code: Angels and Demons.*
Oh, and a little juggernaut called *Spider Man*

Now, don't get me wrong, David's a swell guy. He really is. He's also extremely rich and phenomenally successful in Hollywood. And because we both began our careers at exactly the same time, neck and neck, it has been an unavoidable trap for me to compare my level of success to his. I won't document the comparison for you. Let's just say that in terms of money and power and Hollywood success: I don't measure up.

Let's face it, there's always going to be someone who's more accomplished either professionally or aesthetically—or both—than you are. So get over it.

But wait. Hold on a second... that's the answer?

Don't ask me. Writing is hard, provides no guarantees, involves suffering, and occasionally, if you're lucky and/or exceptionally talented, you hit pay dirt.

What does it mean to hit pay dirt with your writing?

Ah, glad you brought that up.

To me, "Aesthetic Ambition" is an oxymoron. So instead, I decided to divide and conquer. Aesthetic <u>versus</u> Ambition.

I don't believe that aesthetic requires ambition. It requires being true to yourself, discipline, rigor, talent—but it's all a mysterious, highly personal internal process. Ambition, on the other hand, relates to <u>external</u> validation, achievement, accessibility, and success out in the world.

Aesthetic ambition. Let's break it down: My aesthetic is to be brutally honest and self-disclosing to elicit a combination of empathy, pity, and scorn. My ambition is to impress you. I want your praise and respect. I want my speech to be better received than the other two keynote speeches. I want to win.

Let me start again. Find another way in. And then it'll all seamlessly coalesce and come full circle in the end.

Never mind that I'm already in way over my head. I've never written myself into a corner that I haven't been able to write myself out of—and be better for it. I tell my students and colleagues that fiction is always fixable. You can always revise, simplify, change the back story, find a different aesthetic approach. Here goes...

There is no greater joy for a writer than the joy of writing a graceful sentence...with the possible exception of being paid $350,000. For a screenplay written on spec in a three-way bidding war between rival studios.

The 350K can be used as the down payment on a house. The graceful sentence can be used as a building block to create a personally meaningful body of work. So... given the two options (graceful sentence, big bucks) which one is more valuable?

Of course, you might immediately ask: are these two options mutually exclusive? And I might respond with the fact that the box office champ for the past few weeks has been *Paul Blart: Mall Cop*. Emblematic of easily digestible, unchallenging, escapist entertainment during these hard times.

This, while the much more personal, deeper, provocative, nuanced indies are perched precariously far below the top ten mark...and in today's economic climate, clinging for dear life in any studio's business model.

Now, there are exceptions. There are always exceptions. Dark horses. Sleeper hits, such as *Slumdog Millionaire* and *Little Miss Sunshine*. And I won't get into that right now. But these are few and far between. Anomalies. Suffice it to say, for me, there has always been the disparity between art and commerce, the vacillation between being picky and discerning, and being an eager sellout—dare I say, hack?

In this regard, one of my under-employed screenwriter friends keeps insisting to me that she would happily sell out, cash in, take the money and run. Unfortunately, in her case, much to her consternation, the trouble is: no one ever offers her the opportunity to sell out. So she fell into the trap of selling herself short, and only focusing on what I believe are all the wrong questions:

What is commercial?
What's currently performing well at the box office?
What would be the easiest sell at a studio?

Mistakes (to me) because she's attempting to follow trends instead of blazing her own trail.

She's conjuring up more of the same instead of something uniquely her own.

She's prognosticating the marketplace instead of being a storyteller.

She's reading *Daily Variety* instead of reading literature.

She's looking for inspiration in all the wrong places.

She's calculating how to sell the next "high concept" hit instead of inventing new characters that are complex and indelible.

She's focusing on ambition at the expense of her personal aesthetic or a story she feels personally compelled to tell.

She's playing creative Lotto with the odds stacked against her, and if she doesn't make the sale, get the deal, "win" (in her eyes), she's left with the empty promise she's made to herself based on the lie that all she wanted to make was money...when the truth is what she truly wanted was creative fulfillment.

Which brings me to this question: What's worse, financial bankruptcy or creative bankruptcy?

Or to put it another way: Is money the ultimate validation for a writer, or is it more valuable to create a (subjective) "high quality" labor of love that can resonate and impact audiences for years to come?

I've battled and lived with depression for most of my life, and I've come to realize or suspect that it's inextricably linked to my aesthetic ambition, whether or not I'm living up to my artistic potential or just treading water. I've started to wonder if depression might be my inner barometer—a sort of checks and balances—between the delusion that everything I write is precious and golden...and the converse: that everything I write is a steaming pile of dog shit.

So here's another question: can a writer be unsatisfied with a work until he's paid a large sum of money for it...at which point said work magically ascends and becomes brilliant? Aren't we all always waiting for permission to feel good enough about our work and about ourselves?

We all want our work to achieve some form of notoriety, don't we? We all want to be the best in our chosen fields. We all want to be finished with the latest draft and have at least three people we highly respect tell us we've nailed it. Wow! Awesome! Good for you! And it doesn't count if one of these three people is your mother.

We all want to achieve so that we can then...what? Rest on our laurels?

Of course, we all know that resting on laurels is only a temporary respite. Over time, the good goes bad. Like milk, it expires. And the ego (and your agent, if you have one) keeps asking: what's next?

What's next?

When and if this happens, you need to fight against the tendency to try to cannibalize yourself by replicating your former achievement. More of the same won't stretch you creatively, abate your ego, or scratch the itch of your Muse.

And then there are the inevitable comparisons to be made by your Greek Chorus that it's just not as good as your last work...and suddenly you're competing against yourself in the worse possible way...and, trust me on this one, you'll hate yourself for it and feel like a total imposter because that earlier work was a happy accident, emerged in a fever, probably wasn't all that good in the first place, and now you're like an addict needing another fix of adulation. Another gold star.

And now you're mad that your ambition has placed you in this unenviable position of reaching for a higher aesthetic, but your ego keeps kicking the ladder out from under you...so you can't gain any traction.

[Sigh]...when my ego is hungry, all bets are off. It'll devour the good, embellish the bad, and never be satisfied until someone else anoints the new work—with praise, respect, and mostly: money. Sorry. Even then, my ego will label it a "pyrrhic victory" because the ego is always suspicious and will deviously convince me (it won't be hard) that it was a fluke. Bottom line: unworthy.

I've been a member of the Writers Guild of America for 22 years, and with very few exceptions during those years, my professional ambition has surpassed my creative aesthetic. For me, the quality of my output has always been substantially worse when I've been paid in advance to write. The reason: when they're paying me, and I'm a writer for hire, I'm eager to please them more than I'm eager to please myself. Or, in prison parlance, I become their bitch.

Absent deadlines and fiduciary responsibility, I feel freer to experiment, take detours, and fuck up. And it seems that it's only when I fuck up that I manage to have a breakthrough that elevates the work from pedestrian "assignment fulfillment" into a genuine sense of artistic accomplishment.

The major difference here is writing a script based on my own need to tell a story versus writing a story to fulfill somebody else's need to generate a hit project and to impress their boss and their boss' boss. When writing for hire, there are always lots of meetings to determine if everyone involved is creatively "in sync." Another way to put this is: "Are we all on the same page?"

This is very dangerous. It's one form of terror for a writer to face the blank page; it's another terror altogether for a writer to face a page overpopulated by the input from studio executives, producers, agents, and/or actors.

The page becomes too crowded. There's barely any room to type. Writing then becomes an exercise in giving them what they want. The only trouble seems to be that they don't quite know what they want until they read the finished draft...and their bosses like it or lump it.

You might ask: if that's the case, then why not always write on spec and remain true to your singular, aesthetic voice?

Well, simple: it's the economy, stupid. That's an easy catchall for today's recession. Truth be told, I've been using that excuse during good and bad times to chase after the next deal for the sake of monetary validation—and approval from my family and friends. In some families, the old adage "any thing worth doing is worth doing well." In my family, that's been supplanted by "if you're not making money doing it, then it's not worth doing."

When I've written on spec with a singular creative vision that has generated income, I got the ephemeral buzz of pride and accomplishment...

but would have just as rapidly traded it in to the highest bidder. My rationale would be: I can always take the money to feed my bank account and then write something new to feed my soul.

But when that new work was completed, I'm not so sure I wouldn't sell out all over again. I'm incorrigible.

Okay, now let me get down to what I'm really getting at here. What We Talk About When We Talk About Aesthetic Ambition: Me vs. David Koepp.

A couple of years ago my 8-year-old son came up to me and said, "Daddy, I tell my friends that you wrote *Spider Man*."

And I said: "But you know that's not true."

Him: "But your friend in New York wrote it. You know him."

Me: "But that's very different than if I wrote it."

Him: "I know. But I tell them anyway."

And I leave it at that.

I shared this heartwarming story with a good friend of mine in L.A., an A-list TV director. And after she stopped laughing, she told me: "Who cares. Koepp's movies suck. You're a much better writer than he is."

Comparing the state of your career to those of other writers is highly inadvisable. Okay: deadly. Of course I envy Mr. Koepp's professional success. But, more than that, I admire and aspire to achieve his work ethic. I don't know anyone who works harder than he does. Yes, he's been incredibly lucky. He's also incredibly talented and knows how to write for mass audiences. Knows how to make studio heads feel confident and secure about investing hundreds of millions of dollars in one of his screenplays. He's got an unprecedented track record. They know he can deliver. He exudes confidence and competence. Rather than comparing and/or tearing down the aesthetic abilities of others to justify your own relative success—or lack thereof, it's much more useful to focus on your own creative process and evolution as an artist.

I'd like to tell you: go for only the aesthetic! Forget about ambition. But I can't. I'm hardwired for ambition. I need it. I'm gay; I'm Jewish; I'm scrappy and hungry for approval. I have something to prove. I need to make a living. I don't want to be a starving artist. I still haven't ruled out the possibility of winning an Oscar, Emmy, or Tony. I would love to achieve all of this—and more! It would be even better if it all came really easily to me. But it won't. It will require blood, sweat, tears, and infinite patience.

My ambition is here to stay. My aesthetic is constantly evolving. I am a perpetual work-in-progress. Like everything I've ever written or will write.

So the best way I can sum up is: write every day and create the space for wonder. A day when I can sit down with a goal to accomplish on the page—such as establishing form and function in the story—and still find myself immersed in the work to such a degree that I'm making discoveries...is a beautiful day. When the words take on a life of their own, I try to get out of the way.

I believe all writers have these enlightened moments. When I'm truly "in the zone," the ambition part just drops away—along with time and space—and it's all about language, raw emotion, the joy of the graceful sentence.

And the only audience to please is myself.

—Delivered February, 2009, Port Townsend, Washington

PLAYING BY EAR
By Michael Klein

There's a Yamaha grand piano in the basement of the music building at Goddard College that's always in tune. Unusual—that in-tuneness—because with the small resident population on campus, I can't imagine the piano gets played very much. I play it, though. The first thing I do when I get to Vermont for an MFA residency is go to that piano and fall into his arms. Because he's a Yamaha with a tone less strident than some Steinways I've known, he's a great instrument, a transmogrifier. He makes you sound better than you really are.

As it happens, I play mostly by ear—even after years of music theory at Music and Art High School in New York. I play by ear because I seem to wander up and down that black-and-white boulevard of keys in a rapture my education couldn't completely hold me in. The piano seems more reliable when I forget how I know it. Improvisation has been, for me anyway, an activity of a heart—not a mind—amazed it can come up with the next phrase of music. Knowing the names of the notes doesn't lead me on as much as remembering how the notes sound. The same holds true for writing.

I never did formally learn how to write. And before I took it on as a practice, I began the adventure of falling in and out of time through language with a feeling—blatant as daylight—that I could only stay in the world by leaving it occasionally. Physical reality couldn't entice me. Trees, for instance, didn't interest me nearly as much as whatever it was rustling those leaves—the thing they represented. The world is too much with us.

Not knowing what it was in those leaves, but believing in it anyway, led me to poetry. I'd read a lot of poetry and knew it was beautiful in a way nothing else was beautiful. Poetry, from the very beginning, was simply the best truth in a time when there wasn't very much truth, or even very much beauty.

Of course, I was impractical in my youth. And speech-impaired. I was also a burgeoning addict living with parents who were similarly caught between wanting to live and wanting to die. The reading and writing of poems lit up my childhood. And along with the light, something miraculous was happening to time. It kept disappearing in long, inspiring strokes. My first moment of real freedom came the day I couldn't sleep until I finished this:

> Weary people walk the streets
> like shadows not quite real
> where are they going, I wonder?
> Maybe to the harbor, to see the lonely ships
> dark and misty like their own lost dreams.

It's a lousy poem, but one in which I was engaged with a consciousness of difference—empathy for someone, or something, that was outside my own experience—which felt important. I didn't identify with those weary people, per se, but I was engaged when they were engaged—down at the harbor of the metaphors.

Years after following shadows down to the water, and only after I stopped drinking, I got the courage to send work to magazines and eventually started getting published. One day, during a cup of coffee at Lincoln Center, a mentor came into my life—someone who thought my work was more valuable than I did.

My mentor happened to be a poet whose work I loved. I was lucky. She was also someone who was incredibly free, which meant, to an uninformed onlooker like me, that she had summers off (she was a teacher) and went places in her car. We drove up to Vermont in August of 1989 to meet Mark Doty because I was editing a book of poems about AIDS and I'd been told by a number of people that Mark had written a thrilling first book of poems that I should consider for the anthology. While we were visiting, my mentor told me that I should attend the graduate school where Doty was teaching, and I took her advice, whether I believed in it at the time or not, or whether I could even afford it or not. I went to Vermont College, and from there to Provincetown, where I lived on a fellowship at the Fine Arts Work Center in 1990.

I have to say that, after the degree, that fellowship to a town where I had never been was the single most important thing that happened to me. Provincetown was more important than getting published or knowing if I could make a living as a writer, which I thought of a lot because I was broke at the time. But being broke can put you in a state of nervous ecstasy because instead of money your labor only gives back love. I was in love, too, with time in which nothing was required of me—time, whose only reminder came out of a steeple bell from the Universalist church in town. And, in that first winter of another life, I was in love with another person—a painter with red hair. I'd forgotten about red hair as much as I'd forgotten about the sea. We went to Herring Cove and after long walks on the beach we let wind rock the car. I kept thanking God for Provincetown and the man with red hair and for being given seven months at the edge of the sea to have nothing but ideas because they were all I could afford.

I lived in an apartment too far from the water to actually see the bay but I could hear it each night and that sound, along with the foghorn skimming over everything helped me write my first book of poems which went on to be published and win an award. The award didn't give me any more success than I'd already had, which wasn't very much, but it didn't matter. I knew there was something very new, writing-wise, waiting for me after that first book of poetry.

In my second year of living in ecstasy (I got a job in a restaurant so I could stay in Provincetown once my fellowship year was over), I started working on a memoir because the story I wanted to tell couldn't be told in poetry. I didn't know why that was except that the poems I'd tried writing about a seven-year period on the racetrack weren't very good. They were much too lovey-dovey about horses. The memoir, I'd decided, had to be different from what I was used to writing. But, like the foghorn over the sea, poetry would be part of it somehow.

I've realized recently that I write right up to the edge of utterly resisting what I've written. I'm never satisfied. And in the process of putting sentences together, a subject I didn't start with begins to emerge, like Nessie rising out of the Loch. I fight the monster, I acquiesce to it. I rewrite the scene, and set a place for the monster at the table. And there, in revision, writing takes me not where I want to go, but where it wants me to go. With each new draft, the writing keeps taking over more and more because it knows how to make me disappear.

After a few hours of that, I get on the phone. I've been away. I miss people. Or I rent movies. Old movies. And black-and-white stories lately about outer space. Not the Martian stuff, but rather the outer space that drifts dandelionly against the cosmos into the earthly subconscious—those spores that streamed to Earth in the classic film *Invasion of the Body Snatchers.*

If you know the original (it was later made into a very different, but equally scary-as-hell version in the '70's), it's a kind of cinematic treatise about the effect individual thinking has on a world that doesn't recognize or value it. If one were to read between the lines, one could sense a warning here about the danger of art, as well. In the film, a town sleeps its way into conformity through duplication. Someone goes to bed as one persona and wakes up like everyone else—replaced by his deader version: a zombie with no feelings. Conform or be doomed, on the margin, the film seems to say.

Writers have a hard time with conformity because their mission is to resist it. One way of resisting is to make a noise in your writing that rises above the dull tone of one sentence following another sentence—merely telling the story, which always sounds to me like someone talking to himself and not to someone reading what he is saying—not to a reader. There is nothing more deadly than the unrelenting rhythm of what happened next: words parceled out on a conveyor belt of only information. Telling a story isn't enough. You have to make a story happen.

To prevent the dullness of time's moving only in a linear way, it's necessary to put something in the work that is mysterious and remains mysterious—something the writer isn't compelled to explain, explain away. Explain, if you can, the extraordinary conclusion of Joyce's "The Dead." Or the William Maxwell moment in *So Long, See You Tomorrow* where he starts talking about Giacometti. Or, later in the book, when a dog seems to have taken the story in its teeth.

Explain some of the work belonging to William Gass, Jamaica Kincaid, John Ashbery, Annie Proulx, or Sherwood Anderson, for instance. Explain—and please don't—Virginia Woolf's masterpiece *The Waves.* Charles Simic said, "Wonder is becoming a rare emotion," which I think is true. The world gives back a lot of examples (in recent poetry, particularly) of what is rather than what could be.

Surprising yourself, oneself, actually comes from the engagement I unlocked during childhood: with a consciousness of difference. The shock of reading doesn't necessarily happen through finding yourself in the character, but with the character. Empathy. "The love I have known is the love of/two people staring/not at each other, but in the same direction," Frank Bidart says in a poem (and, in this instance, improvising off Antoine de Saint-Exupery). Reading and Writing seem to me to be like those two lovers with an idea about changing the world.

Changing the world begins, of course, in ideas. And getting them doesn't necessarily mean that you have to go out and stack up death-defying experiences to give you more of a sense of being alive. You don't even have to have an interesting life, just one that never stops resisting the what is. The only thing, it seems to me, that we don't resist as writers is the ability to be moved by the singularity of what happens to us—however horrible it may be. Andre Dubus, the extraordinary writer who died at the end of 1998, did his most transporting work after a car accident put him in wheelchair. What the bystander on the highway might have seen as someone else's tragedy, Dubus saw as the work of an angel.

And Emily Dickinson didn't go downstairs very much. But the world and its ideas never stopped streaming into her and through the house where she lived in Amherst, Massachusetts, because she wanted to receive that world. Her ideas were her major experiences and by staying upstairs, she lived, in a sense, above her life. She also knew that living and dying weren't linear but circular—an idea her epitaph bears out: Born: December 1830. Called back: May, 1886.

The artists I know have the capacity for wonder and surprise coursing through their veins. And they are all riotously free—whether they have, the way my mentor had, summers off or not.

—*Delivered 2000, Plainfield, Vermont*
Poets and Writers

IV. Originality and Influence

ORIGINALITY AND CREATIVITY:
CHILDREN OF *BEOWULF* AND TRIMALCHIO
By Jeanne Mackin

"I think I have done something original," F. Scott Fitzgerald wrote to his editor, some years after the first publication of *The Great Gatsby* had already been deemed a publishing failure. Three hundred copies of the novel moldered in a warehouse and Fitzgerald died soon after, believing his books would be buried with him. But that's a different story. I want to talk about the originality of *The Great Gatsby* and what Fitzgerald might have meant by his claim for it.

Originality certainly doesn't shine in the plot: Jay Gatsby is a Midwestern farm boy who runs away from a suffocating, low-class home, joins the army, finds girl, loses girl, hooks up with a wealthy criminal, ends up in a mansion on Long Island hosting glitzy parties for the rich and infamous, and then is shot to death in his swimming pool. The novel's first layer asks us to believe that Jay dies for love of Daisy, the girl who gave up waiting and married her daddy's choice instead. Tom Buchanan is not a bootlegger, but his crime is organized nonetheless, in the offices on Wall Street where the narrator, Nick Carraway, is a youngster learning the ways of this world, and love, ultimately has little to do with it.

Jay and Daisy are lovers in the old tradition, passionate about each other but separated by circumstances and the proverbial dissenting families. It is Romeo and Juliet and dozens of others of unhappy love stories, and Fitzgerald knew it.

In addition to being a Romeo and a Christ figure (several times Fitzgerald refers to Gatsby as the son of God, the man who will die for our sins), Gatsby is also a twentieth century incarnation of Trimalchio from *The Satyricon*, Petronius's collection of stories about the decadence of Nero's Rome, theorized as the first novel in western literature. Fitzgerald's working title for the novel, in fact, was *Dinner with Trimalchio*: a modern retelling of Trimalchio's feast, those wild nights of eat, drink and be merry, for tomorrow we die. The parties Gatsby gives at his pretentious mansion are direct descendants of those wild parties, with their conspicuous consumption, drunken revelers, characters of questionable class and occupation, and a general sense of society going to hell in a hand basket, as it did under Nero, and as Fitzgerald saw it doing in the early 1920's.

Fitzgerald's characters parallel Petronius's characters: the young narrator living hand to mouth, an outside commentator who wants to be an insider; Trimalchio, Jay's ancestor, the false gentleman with bad grammar and questionable taste and lower class origins, and all the others, the deceiving husbands, gold-diggers, criminals and wannabees of Nero's Rome and 1920's New York.

The Satyricon is also home to the tale of the Ephesian Matron, a grieving widow who lets herself be comforted a little too easily. Daisy grieves for Jay Gatsby twice, first when he leaves for the war and then at the end of the novel, when he is shot by the wrong jealous husband for the wrong crime. Both times, Daisy is easily comforted by Tom Buchannan; even grief becomes a commodity to acquire and dispose of. The Ephesian Matron, as a theme and character, is not original even to Petronius; she appeared earlier in ancient folk stories and has reappeared steadily through the centuries in the tales of La Fontaine, as the Wife of Bath, the carpe diem poets, and thousands of others of somewhat shady female characters right down to Scarlet O'Hara and beyond.

So the plot isn't a new one, and the characters aren't original. Yet *Gatsby* is a great novel, both creative and original. Why? Largely because *The Satyricon* is humorous, in a corrupt and decadent kind of way; *Gatsby* is not. It's deadly serious.

This, then, was a part of Fitzgerald's creativity: the work he began as satire was revised into a modern tragedy. He sensed with that extra faculty that made him a great writer, that the tale, told in the twentieth century, was not going to be, or perhaps did not need to be, funny. He did not discover this immediately but in the act of revision; early versions of *Gatsby* were humorous and satirical. (One of them, *Trimalchio: An Early Version of The Great Gatsby*, was published by Cambridge University Press in 2000.)

I also suspect a large part of Fitzgerald's creativity, what made his Trimalchio/Gatsby different from the ones that went before, was that

Fitzgerald was a master of structure. Earlier versions of this tale were kinds of iliads, or series of stories, meant to be told night after night like courses at dinner, related but separate. Fitzgerald's structure is so tight it could hold several oceans without leaking. No element of plot or character or setting can be considered extraneous, not even the billboard bearing the faded eyes of Doctor T.J. Eckleburg that "brood on over the solemn dumping ground."

Perhaps even more importantly, what also makes this novel of Fitzgerald's original is that while it talks back to its elders, to Petronius and Chaucer and Shakespeare and Benjamin Franklin and Keats and Wharton and dozens of other writers on Fitzgerald's book shelf, it also speaks forward. It makes the same old story as much a part of the future as the past. Another working title of Fitzgerald's novel was *The Death of the American Dream*. Decades later, S. Hunter Thompson gave one of his novels a working title of *Death of the Red, White and Blue*. It was later published as *Fear and Loathing in Las Vegas* and Thompson based his novel on *The Great Gatsby*.

"The merit of originality is not novelty, it is sincerity," Thomas Carlyle wrote in the nineteenth century, and that perhaps was Fitzgerald's true genius: the obvious sincerity of the work. He believed in that story, as old as it was, believed in it enough to make it new again. His novel becomes about Black Friday, the American financial meltdown of 1929: "They were careless people, Tom and Daisy—they smashed up things and creatures and then retreated back into their money or their vast carelessness or whatever it was that kept them together, and let other people clean up the mess they had made..." But he finished the novel in 1924, five years before the beginning of the Great Depression (fourteen years before Bernie Madoff was born). In writing of what had been, Fitzgerald wrote about what was to come. Truly creative work has this quality of prophecy.

Another tale told over and over appeared in this generation as *Grendel*, by John Gardner, based on the old Anglo Saxon text of *Beowulf*. Just as *The Satyricon* is recognized as the beginning of the western novel, *Beowulf* is recognized as the beginning of the popular novel, that is, a novel written in the vernacular, the language of the people, the plowman and weavers and bakers and ditch diggers, not the language of the rulers, the kings and priests. *Beowulf* is the first novel written to be read by common folk.

The premise of this ancient story is as old as the embodied idea of *The Great Gatsby*, the idea of grabbing all you can and leaving other people to clean up. In *Beowulf*, a people, small and primitive but not knowing they are small or primitive, are invaded by a more powerful people, and edged into a fringe of nowhere, with considerable bloodshed, because not even the innocent or naïve want to live in a fringe of nowhere when they once had their own. *Beowulf* is a story of conquest, and of the mortality of both heroes and civilizations.

Gardner's version of *Beowulf* is not written from the hero's point of view but the monster's, just as *The Great Gatsby* is written not from the winner's point of view, but the loser's. Originality is often not in the plotting, but in the revelation of plot.

Gardner knew that the idea of oppression and tragedy is too large to look away from, especially when it has embodied itself in a personal tragedy, as it did for Gardner. But look at the lineage of this novel, and you'll see how omnipresent the original is, and how extensive the creative can become.

Gardner's *Grendel* is about humankind in general and in specifics, that tendency of our species to move ever westward, following a setting rather than rising sun, the westward move from India to Europe and the watery journey over water to the unknown continent still known as the new world, and then home again, to the far east. The western move is indicative of our restlessness, our curiosity, our greed for more, always more. The western migration that is history (Fitzgerald, through Nick Carraway, describes the horrific first world war as "that delayed Teutonic migration known as the Great War") is marked by bloody conquest. Gardner chose to tell this story from the point of view of the conquered, and in the 1960's, when Gardner was working on this novel, when the U.S. was fighting in Vietnam, that was an important distinction.

But *Grendel* is also an ancient love story, in the style of *Beauty and the Beast*, *Caliban and Miranda*; it is the story of the impossible love of beauty by the monstrous, and Gardner's version does exactly what this old story requires us to do: reconsider what is monstrous, and what is beautiful. It's an important discussion when you are talking about invasion and conquering, because the conqueror's justification is always one of superiority over the conquered.

Grendel, besides being well written, even beautifully written, represents that ongoing conversation between writers of all centuries, a kind of call and response that keeps literature alive and moving: *Beowulf*, and so Gardner's *Grendel* is one of the oldest stories we have, saying simply, "I took it because I could, because you could not keep it." It can be traced to *The Book of Genesis*: the happy Adam and Eve invaded by the cunning serpent and then outcast, but the story predates even the Abrahamic matter, disappears into a vanishing horizon of history and narrative and becomes the second most common idea embodied in literature, second only to stories of birth and becoming. After birth and becoming there is death, and the story of *Grendel* is the story of death.

Beowulf is also one of the newest stories. It has appeared, in this generation, in an opera by Julie Taymor, in several movies and in a Michael Crichton bestseller; the more subtle works of print literature that tell this story of invasion and the conquered probably can't be counted. A good story, a true story, simply can't be told too often, but what makes the repetition important is that call and response, that sense of communication and redirection that fosters originality even in retelling.

A.S. Byatt, in her essay "Old Tales, New Forms" (and if you are uncertain about what the old tales are, read Roberto Calasso's *The Marriage of Cadmus and Harmony*) describes this process of retelling as:

the slow piling one on top of the other of thin transparent layers which constitute the most appropriate picture of the way in which the perfect narrative is revealed...the novel could almost be said to record the metamorphosis of authored stories into the plain, negotiable coin of the fund of generally available motifs and anecdotes.

I'm sure, given the embodied ideas in *The Great Gatsby*...boy doesn't get girl, greed is destructive, etc., etc., ...that thousands of writers are at work, right now, of a 2009 version of this story. Some of them will be very good, maybe one or two will be new masterpieces. The best will, like *Gatsby* and *Grendel*, look forward, be action rather than reaction, because while creativity is a backward glance over the shoulder, back to the original, it then looks forward, to its own descendants, to what is to come. It is paradox rather than simplicity, embodied by Fitzgerald, in the final line of *The Great Gatsby*: "So we beat on, boats against the current, borne back ceaselessly into the past."

I'm not saying there is nothing new under the sun. It's already been said. I'm repeating it. There is nothing new under the sun. There is only you, the writer, looking to embody an old idea in a new way. Idea is the original. We are the creative. Creativity is not a mere matter of novelty, though large leaps are made, some of them sometimes novel; creativity is that boat beating against the ancient, ageless current.

That there is an original should not deter our creativity. In fact it is in recognizing the original that we learn to go beyond it, into the creative. "Ordinary happiness," A.S. Byatt says, "is to be outside a story, full of curiosity, looking before and after." That describes, perhaps, the ultimate relationship of originality and creativity.

—*Delivered Summer, 2009, Plainfield, Vermont*

ORIGINALITY AND INFLUENCE
By Jane E. Wohl

My thoughts on this topic begin with the Tower Bridge in London. We all know what it looks like; it's as much a part of the tourist kitsch as plastic Statues of Liberty in New York. We can find the bridge on tea towels, on pencils, on placemats.

I first saw the real bridge ten years ago with three Wyoming teenagers with whom I had spent the day roaming around London. Michael really wanted to see the Tower Bridge at night, so we found our way there. We asked a passer-by to take our picture with each of our cameras, and so now we all have copies of this moment. I saw the Tower Bridge most recently in May of 2009 when I drove over it in a taxi and then, the next day, went under it by boat. So, now in my own mind, I have several different versions of the bridge with a long string of associations with each one. I think of the bridge, and I think of Michael, who is now a graduate student at Columbia, I think of Ryan who directs his church choir in Sheridan, Wyoming and I think of Anne, who is now a mother working on a degree in music therapy, and, at the same time, I think of the perfect day when I glided beneath the bridge by boat, in London all by myself and cherishing the solitude. I also think, as I did in that boat, about Dickens' story *Our Mutual Friend*, which is really a meditation on life on and around the Thames. None of these strings of images and associations has anything to do with the ubiquitous tea towels, pencils, or placements...

However, at the same time, these strings of associations are also inseparable from the cliché because if I see a placemat or tea towel, the blurry image sets off my own associations. I am incapable of separating the kitsch from the memories.

Ecclesiastes 1:9 tells us that, "What has been will be again, what has been done will be done again; there is nothing new under the sun." In contrast, but in a very different chronological time, Ezra Pound commanded that writers "Make it new."

Is it possible to hold both these ideas in our heads at once? It's a little like looking at a Necker cube, where one face comes forward and then retreats without our conscious mind willing it.

As I began to think about what I wanted to say today, I began thinking about the words "originality" and "influence."

Initially, my first reading of the two words was that one is concerned with being "original" being unique, being "new" and the other is concerned with those outside pressures that push against being "original," but then the Necker cube began to flip in my head.

I recently learned that a word that contains two contradictory meanings is called a contronym (thanks to the same Michael with whom I saw the bridge). Think about the word "cleave." It means to cling to, and also to split from. How can a word do that?

Think about the word "dust": It means to sprinkle particles on (as in dusting of snow) and it also means to remove those fine particles. Consider "sanction," which means both to allow and to penalize.

I want to think about this concept in connection to the word "originality." On the one hand, it means the ability to "create something new," "creating something that is not a replica of something else"; however, if we think the word "origin" which means source, or beginning of something, then "originality" can also mean the connection to that source. So, here's place where my mind vibrates back and forth like the cube. Do I create something new, or do I demonstrate my connections to the "origins," the beginnings by the work I do? Is *Ecclesiastes* right? Is there really nothing new under the sun? Or is what I create unique and new? Or is it some weird combination of both?

How does this concept of the contronym apply to "influence"?

It means "a power, person or thing that changes the course of events," but it comes from the Latin "to flow" and one of the secondary meanings implies that influence flows into events or people without their control, as in the word "confluence," which means where two things flow into each other, as in the confluence of the Missouri and Mississippi Rivers. If we cannot control the "influences" in our lives, how can we control what we "create"? How can we be "original"?

It seems to me that the question of "influence" is especially pertinent in connection to recent comments by and about Sonia Sotomayor about being a Latina woman. What the critics of her remarks forget or purposely deny is that none of us, white, black, male, female, Latina, Anglo, is free of "influence." No one can convince me that John Roberts or Samuel Alito makes his decisions in an "influence-free" environment. They have been subject to "influence" exactly the same way any of us has been. What is important is learning to recognize those influences. What flows into us, into our lives, into our perceptions and understandings of the world without our control, without our own consciousness? Some of those influences are so deeply embedded in our psyches that we do not notice them. Why, for example, do some people feel nervous in enclosed spaces and others feel uncomfortable in large open areas? Sometimes there's a specific origin, identifiable trigger to those reactions, but sometimes there is not.

Consider W.G. Sebald's novel *Austerlitz,* in which the narrator relates how he listens, for much of the novel, to the character Austerlitz unraveling the mysteries of his life. Austerlitz discovers a past that was unknown to him for much of his life, yet, through his narrative, the reader can see how this past influenced Austerlitz in ways that he neither recognized nor understood. I know that every time I have reread *Austerlitz* I have reconsidered memory, thought about the tricks psychological repression plays on our understandings of the world, and reflected on the influence that historical events beyond our control have on our lives.

This novel is, among other things, an exploration of those ways in which we are influenced. (I use the passive voice intentionally here.) If we "are influenced" and have little control over those influences, how can we be "original"? We will be writing, creating and acting from a place we don't understand, controlled by outside influences. But, for me, this is too mechanistic a view of creativity. If we are simply the victims of "influences," then we really have no control over what we do or how we act, and the writings, the art of creation, contradicts that notion.

T.S. Eliot, in his essay "Tradition and the Individual Talent," writes about exactly this conundrum: "No poet, no artist of any art, has his complete meaning alone, and this is conformity between the old and the new. Whoever has approved this idea of order, of the form of European, of English literature, will not find it preposterous that the past should be altered by the present as much as the present is directed by the past." Eliot warns us that we need to aware of our predecessors, we must know the past, but we also must not simply replicate the past. But he also talks about the mutability of the past, the way the past is changed by the present.

There are several paintings which clearly illustrate the way the past and present interact. In 1650, the Spanish painter Velasquez painted a portrait of Pope Innocent X. This portrait shows the pontiff in ceremonial dress, looking rich and powerful. This painting is famous enough that most people can see it in their minds' eyes, but almost any mental image of a wealthy, powerful 17th Century man will do. This portrait is, for my purposes, the "original." Three hundred years later, the English painter, Francis Bacon, painted a work called *Study after Velasquez*. This painting is clearly a reflection on the Velasquez because the person in the Bacon painting is sitting in a similar fashion and wears similar robes, specifically the rich purple mantle; however, Bacon has distorted the man's face so that it looks like the man in screaming in agony, and he has painted bars from the top to the bottom of the painting so that it appears that the person is imprisoned. Clearly, this is not just a copy of the Velasquez, but it raises the following questions:

Which of these paintings is original? What are their origins? What are their influences? Where does one painting become separate from the other? I think this is a wonderful example of what Eliot says about the way the past and the present interact and change each other.

Once we have seen the Bacon painting, we cannot look at the Velasquez in the same way again. On its own the Velasquez portrait is that of a powerful, though shifty eyed man, dressed in the finery of his office. Velasquez' Pope looks at the viewer, and while we might not feel any strong kinship to him, we see him as human, as like us, in some ways. The Bacon, through its bold brush strokes, its intentional defamation of the portrait, and its homage to Munch's *The Scream,* makes the viewer consider what it means to negate the past, what means to be codified into an office (Why is Bacon's Pope screaming?). He makes the viewer think about how simple lines of paint can create a jail and a distance between the viewer and the subject. Bacon's Pope is no longer connected to us, the viewers, in the way that Velasquez's is. Bacon has made us rethink our relationship to the first portrait.

I would guess that no one would argue that the Bacon painting is not "original." It is clearly not a copy of something else, the ideas and images are clearly filtered through Bacon's own sensibilities, but the "origins" of the painting are clear (and his title makes clear even if we didn't know the original). The "influences" of the painting are perhaps less clear. I would not say that Velasquez "influenced" Bacon here, although his painting is the "origin" of the Bacon work, but rather that the influences come from somewhere else. The influences in this case could include, and I am speculating here, a disenchantment with the established Catholic church, a reflection of existentialism, and a wish to be iconoclastic, or the influences could be more personal and more subtle than we as viewers will even know.

Visual art provides another example of this complex relationship. The 18th-century Italian artist, Piranesi, created an etching called *Imaginary Prisons.* In this work, stairways move on diagonal through the picture; however, these stairways do not seem to lead anywhere. There is a bridge in the picture that has no access points. It is a rendering of something that cannot really exist, as the title implies. The 20th-century artist, M.C. Escher created a work with stairways that seem to go nowhere, or that change direction in odd ways and lead to places that are not where we expect them, a landing in a vertical line along the side of the painting, for example. Each of these works seems to express a sense of disorientation and misdirection, yet the Escher does not refer directly to the Piranesi work. Has he been influenced? Or has Escher created a work that is original and only resembles the Piranesi because of the similarity of subject matter and design? Is there really nothing new under the sun or is Escher, like Eliot says, reordering the past? No one would seriously accuse Escher of copying Piranesi but the influence is clear. Is one more "original" than the other? Are they both working with ideas that percolate through human culture and thus, influence artists regardless of time?

I want to go back and think about these sets of pictures again because, in my mind, each pair demonstrates something different. The Velasquez is clearly the "origin" of the Bacon work. Bacon uses the Velasquez as the catalyst to create a new work, a different work, but the origin of the Bacon work is clear.

With the Piranesi and the Escher, we don't see the same interplay. These two works are connected, and Escher may have been "influenced" by Piranesi (and I am not enough of an art history scholar to know for sure) but he isn't commenting on the Piranesi work. It's more like Piranesi and Escher are parallel artists, working centuries apart, but side-by-side in their explorations of the absurd and the imaginary. However, no one would confuse these two artists. Their styles are individual, so they may be working with the same ideas (influences? origins?) but they present them in ways that are their own.

As I put together these reflections, I have realized that the connection between these ideas is not simple, that originality cannot be separated from influence, and that we are, by biology, by history, by culture, connected to origins, and those origins influence us in both subtle and obvious ways. It's clear to me that we do not live in an either/or world. It's not a choice between "originality" on one hand, and "influence" on the other, but rather the world of creativity is one in which origins, originality, influence all mix and slosh around together. What influences me will not be the same things that influence you, but what is important, it seems to me, is that we listen to those influences, we think about the moments that push us into something "original," that we act on that impulse to create, and then we let go, and let what we have done become an influence for someone else.

I want to end with thinking again about the Tower Bridge. Once we have thought about the ways the lines intersect and move in the Piranesi and the Escher works, we can't see the Tower Bridge, or even the Brooklyn Bridge the same way. So, is our experience of the bridge less original, less our own because of this? I don't think so. Our understanding of the bridge, the way we see it, will be influenced by what I have just said, but you will still bring your own experience to it, just as our understanding of the Bacon painting is influenced by our observation of the Velasquez painting.

Ecclesiastes is right, there is nothing new under the sun, but so is T.S. Eliot, and so is Ezra Pound. Our task as writers is to make the old into the new. We must recreate (and re-creation implies that something has already been created once) our experience, whether it's on paper or on canvas, so that it becomes new. In recreating our experience, bringing to bear all those influences and original sources, filtering them through our own sensibilities we challenge the old, we re-order the old, we change the way others will see the world. We make it new.

—*Delivered Summer, 2009, Plainfield, Vermont*

WRITING AGAINST CANON, WRITING AGAINST CLICHÉ: CREATING A CANON, BECOMING A CLICHÉ
By Kenny Fries

1. Canon as Cliché
Canon: a rule or especially body of rules or principles generally established as valid and fundamental in a field or art or philosophy:
A group of literary works that are generally accepted as representing a field.

I never had a canon. There has never been a canon of literature about people with disabilities. Or, to be more accurate, the accepted canon of what I most wanted to write about was the opposite of the experience of my life.

The canon of disabled people in literature, though long and luminous, ranging from Sophocles' blinded Oedipus and Shakespeare's Richard III, from Dickens's Tiny Tim and Melville's Ahab to Mary Shelley's Frankenstein's monster, defined disabled people as cripples defined by excess, charity, or villainy. These characters were saints or sinners, the blind man who knows too much, the "feeble-minded" who felt too much (and made us pity too much), the superhuman who achieved too much (and inspired us), the greedy deformed by wanting too much.

More recently, in the 1930s and 1940s, the canon of disabled characters expanded to include characters created by Nathaniel West, Dalton Trumbo, Nelson Algren and Carson McCullers, characters that became stand-ins, metaphors, reflecting the values of being an outsider in society. Later, we have characters such as Bellow's William Einhorn, a character who survives because he, to quote Bellow, "wouldn't stay a cripple...Einhorn, he couldn't hold his soul in it." Pop culture gave us Mr. Magoo, the affable man with a sight impairment who is the butt of jokes and ridicule, as well as the villains of James Bond films and Captain Hook (the signaling of Good vs. Evil by the addition of a hook peg leg, or eye patch; introductory guides to screenwriting actually counsel fledgling authors to give their villain a limp or an amputated limb), Richard III and Ahab redux.

In the 20th century, in the United States, parallel to these fictional characters we had real life actual disabled people who loomed over the canonical images of disability: Franklin Delano Roosevelt and Helen Keller, who both reinscribed the various myths of disability that still pervade our culture, one denied his disability; the other defined by it. (Interestingly, both FDR and Helen Keller became "fictional" characters in the disability-defining dramas and movies, *Sunrise at Campobello* and *The Miracle Worker*. The seductive plot possibilities of the medical model of disability, its emphasis on overcoming and cures are irresistible in creating conventional dramatic structure.)

Even the international art world supplied us with canonical icons, giving us Toulouse-Lautrec in late 19th century Paris and Frida Kahlo in mid-20th century Mexico City. However, because his life doesn't follow the trajectory of the canonical disability plot, notably missing from this starry array, at least until my new book, *The History of My Shoes and the Evolution of Darwin's Theory*, is Henri Matisse, whose late-in-life disability led to his cut-outs, some of the most luminous art of the 20th century, the creation of which is due to Matisse's disability, which did not allow him to continue painting in his usual manner.

What tied all these canonical figures together was that nondisabled writers and critics who viewed disability from without, perpetuated their images, defined by the gaze and the needs of the nondisabled world.

Cliché: from the French verb, clicher, to stereotype.

In the summer of 1989, when I began searching for the words with which to begin speaking about my own experience living with a congenital disability, most of what I found was a canon filled with myths, metaphors, and lies. What I found were stereotypes. What I found were clichés.

I began to take the initial steps of finding the language, unearthing the images, shaping the forms with which I could express an experience I had never read about before, so that my experience as a person with a disability could become meaningful to others. What I remember about that summer of 1989 is wanting to throw all those drafts away, not thinking them poems. Not having a role model in whose steps I could follow, unsure of my own identity as both a writer and as a person who lives with a disability, I felt like a shadow spirit unable to meld successfully on the page the nondisabled world I lived in with my experience of being disabled in that world.

Not only was I writing about my life as a disabled man in a way that transformed this experience so others, disabled and nondisabled alike, could see themselves, but I was also writing about my life as a gay man. Being that a disabled man has been traditionally viewed as asexual, and that a gay man has been traditionally been viewed as overly sexual, this was, luckily, a difficult stereotype to live up to. (When in doubt I always chose the latter since not only does a lot of sex make for better reading but it is usually more fun than celibacy, as well.)

In 1994, I was invited to and participated in the historic "Disability and Performance: A Contemporary Chautauqua" organized by Vicki Lewis, director of Other Voice at the Mark Taper Forum in Los Angeles. That April weekend, prominent artists with disabilities gathered from all across the United States to perform, read, teach, learn, talk, and get to know one another. That we had something valuable to offer was evidenced not only by an audience hungry to share our work, not only by the overcrowded classes, the sold-out performances, the TV cameras from CNN and WNET, but also by the lasting, nurturing relationships forged by many of the participant artists.

When leaving Los Angeles, I did not know that the writing I was exposed to that weekend would eventually form the core of *Staring Back: The Disability Experience from the Inside Out*, the anthology of writers with disabilities I edited and Plume published in 1997. I had unearthed work that, once published, quickly became the canon of contemporary writing about disability by writers with disabilities in the United States. By this time, I had also learned enough and matured enough as a writer to negotiate the spaces within the double-stereotype of being both gay and disabled. My memoir, *Body, Remember*, the first memoir that looked at the life of a gay man with a disability in the United States, was also published in 1997.

2. Cultural Cliché

1. A trite or overused expression or idea
2. A person or character whose behavior is predictable or superficial
3. A trite or obvious remark

The above narrative, even for most of you who are hearing it for the first time, has become, to me, a cliché. This previous narrative is what I am expected to deliver, especially in situations where I am the only visibly disabled writer—and if I don't bring up the subject nobody else will.

So, I want to go beyond the expected and offer another, more recent cross-cultural narrative.

In 2002, I went to Japan as a Creative Arts Fellow of the Japan/US Friendship Commission and the National Endowment for the Arts to look at disability and the life of people with disabilities in Japan. During my seven months in Japan I wrote about Japanese gardens.

On the surface, my original intention and the poems I wrote would seem to have nothing to do with each other: disability and Japanese gardens. And it isn't as though I didn't pursue my goal of finding out as much as I could about disability and the life of disabled people in Japan. I did this. But my writing in Japan, on the surface at least, does not have disability as its subject.

Before arriving in Japan, I had not written a poem in over four years. Years of working first on my memoir, and a new nonfiction book, which looks at Darwin's ideas of evolution from the perspective of disability, made it seem as if a poem could no longer hold as much as I wanted my writing to hold.

But soon after arriving in Japan, a place I had never been before, this changed. I was overwhelmed with an abundant array of new cultural experiences. I was constantly filled with unfamiliar but emotionally encompassing sights and sounds. Among these experiences, two began to pervade my thoughts: the irises of Meiji Jingu and the voice of Japanese singer Mika Kimula.

I began spending more and more time in the gardens of Japan. What began to emerge from these encounters was a sequence of poems that on the surface are about what can actually be found in some of the gardens I visited. However, that is only the surface subject of the poems because Japanese gardens hold within them a microcosm of what it means to be alive in a mortal world. And living life in a mortal world is perhaps the greatest lesson learned from the experience of living with a disability. There is nothing more constant than change.

When I began working on these poems, I was afraid that they would seem too artificially "Oriental," in the manner of say, Puccini's

Madama Butterfly, or Richard Rodgers' "March of the Siamese Children" in the Rodgers and Hammerstein musical *The King and I.* I was somewhat suspect that here I was, a writer from the United States during his first months in Japan writing short, six-line image-focused poems about Japanese gardens. In Japan, I did not want to become like all those nondisabled writers writing about disability from the outside.

But I soon realized that the form of the poems, though similar to haiku and tanka, was also similar to the poems I had begun writing in 1989, the first poems I wrote about disability, and to those composed a year later in *The Healing Notebooks,* my sequence about living with an HIV-positive boyfriend, all of which were collected in my book, *Anesthesia.*

For example, compare the first line from *The Healing Notebooks, #12:*
Begin with scraps of paper, odd
sentences, someone else's phrases—

With the first lines of the third poem of *In the Gardens of Japan,* *Kikugetsutei, Ritsurin Koen,*
Borrow the hills. The algae-filled pond
is the sea; three stones
its islands. To recreate the world, first
take it apart.

The poems I was writing in Japan seemed to be leading me back to where I began when I began writing poems over a decade and a half ago, not only in form but in content, as well. Just as I talked of borrowing other's words in that poem in *The Healing Notebooks,* I was using the Japanese technique of *shakkei,* borrowed scenery, which I mention at the beginning of the poem about Kikugetsutei. In this poem I borrow from an ancient Chinese poem that gives the name to the teahouse of which I am writing: Kikugetsutei, "scooping the moon" teahouse, named for the image in this Chinese poem. And later in the sequence I borrow a famous line from a famous poem by the United States poet Elizabeth Bishop: "Write it before the sake passes by," I write, borrowing the imperative "Write it" from Bishop's last line of her villanelle, "One Art."

As I discovered that these organic creative processes were taking place in the poems I was writing about Japanese gardens I realized that I wasn't engaged in an "Orientalist" process, but something deeper. And realizing this, I wanted to explore how my English words might reverberate if accompanied by the sounds of the ancient Japanese music I was hearing at noh, bunraku, and hogaku. Could the poems I was writing be songs?

The moment I heard the beginning of Yuka Takechi's music for my poems, with antique bells, I knew this composer to whom English was a second language, had keyed into the essence of what I was writing. And when, toward the end of her setting for the first poem, "Irises, Meiji Jingu," there is a pause after the word "pink" and before the word "thought," her music understands the complex nature of the thought process behind the seemingly simple images. It was immediately clear that somehow this composer from Japan understood this work from this untranslated writer from the United States on a deep level. The result reminded me of the feelings I had as a "shadow spirit" when I first began writing about disability in 1989. But now I was no longer straddling the world of the nondisabled and the disabled. I was straddling the cultures of Japan and the United States, East and West, what was old but new to me, and new but old to my Japanese collaborators.

My time in Japan had brought me back to a place I had not been in a long time. Just as so many Japanese gardens lead you from their entrance, through various meanderings, back to where you began, my encounters with Japan and my risking a cultural cliché led me back to poems, which, like the gardens of which I write, seem to hold within them, an entire world.

3. Footnote

Canon is a word derived from a Hebrew and Greek word denoting a reed or cane. Therefore it means something straight, or something to keep straight. Very interesting for a writer who both uses a cane and is decidedly not straight, as we have come to understand the word. It seems that I'm always coming up against a stereotype in conflict with itself.

—*Delivered Summer, 2004, Plainfield, Vermont*

BEWARE OF OTHERS

By Susan Kim

Graduates—my heartfelt congratulations. You've worked hard to get here and in return for your efforts, you leave today with a bunch of stuff. You get a new degree, a Master of Fine Arts—something that's impressive and often useful. You get a commemorative badge. You leave with a creative thesis that I sincerely hope will have a life beyond Goddard. You also leave with essays, papers, and forty five annotations that God alone knows what you're going to do with. And last but not least, you get to leave with some advice, from me...free of charge.

First off, let me say that I don't usually like to give advice. This may seem odd coming from an advisor, an advisor who has in fact given quite a few of you many, many pages of advice, and not all of it welcome. To this, I say: a foolish consistency is the hobgoblin of little minds. Besides, I'm enough of a traditionalist to think that this occasion merits something special, and enough of a dramatist to want to provide an 11th hour number, no matter how humble.

One of the problems with advice is that often, like other examples of bad writing, it's too vague. This happens when the speaker tries to reach heights of inspiration while appealing to the broadest audience possible...and this, as any playwright can tell you, is not what you'd call a playable action. So advice-givers often take the opposite approach. They stick to the specific and tell you to floss your teeth and wear sunscreen. The late actor David Carradine—best known for his role as the strangely un-Asian-looking Shaolin priest in the TV series *Kung Fu*, as well as for his recent accidental death by autoerotic asphyxiation— had apparently been a font of such advice. My two favorites are "never marry a woman named Candy" and "never buy anything from a man who's out of breath." But advice like this, while memorable and even useful, is not inspirational. Nor is it especially relevant to you, the MFA graduating class. It isn't *advice geared towards writers*.

I tried to come up with some advice that would be appropriate for a barn-full of writers, advice that was practical, specific and germane. Here are the first things I thought of: 1, save all your drafts; 2, back up your files; and 3, try not to breathe in that weird toner smell when you're printing out, because who knows what that stuff is doing to your lungs, anyway?

But that's not what I want to tell you. I want to tell you to *watch out for other people.*

I realize this sounds weird and paranoid, not to mention rude, since most of you are in fact surrounded by other people right now, many of them dear to your heart. I'm not really talking about them. I'm talking about *feedback*—not the feedback you received here at Goddard, which was of course impeccable, but the kind you will encounter as you continue onwards with your writing life, if that's where you choose to go. I hope you realize that as a writer, you are in a sense placing your hands and feet in the public stocks, where passersby will feel free to insult and harass you. You are signing on for a lifetime of feedback from not only editors, agents, publishers, producers, artistic directors, literary managers, reviewers, critics and academics, but also friends, family, neighbors and colleagues.

You'll also be getting an earful from strangers. As you may have already experienced, people who don't know you from Adam will nevertheless have no compunction coming up to you after a reading or emailing you out of the blue to tell you what they thought of your work. They offer suggestions on what to trim, what to clarify, what to change. Some will helpfully suggest the names of other writers who did it better than you. Sometimes, they say things that make you feel great, and sometimes, they say things that make you want to kill yourself...and them. Sometimes, they even make sense. But no matter what anyone says, whether it warms your heart or chills your bowels, proceed at your own risk. *Beware of others.*

At the end of each residency, advisors toss out ideas for workshops they want to offer and I always thought I'd like to do something on how to respond to feedback. Since I work a lot in television, I was especially taken by the idea of a workshop called "How to Handle Incomprehensible Notes from Idiots in Expensive Sweaters." (I also played with the thought of a workshop on "Dealing with Rejection," a lab on Writers' Block, and a master class in Failure. Perhaps these should be offered as degree requirements in the future).

I never did get around to offering my workshop, but I will give you its gist, the accumulated nacre that forms the pearl of my wisdom. Are you ready for it? Here it is: everyone has an agenda.

People want things. They want to keep their jobs, they want to seem smart and perceptive, they want to be valued. They want to help, they want to hurt, they want to flatter or be flattered, they want to be remembered. This is as it should be; want is action, action is life, and if people didn't want anything, we'd all be dead. But when someone is responding to your work when it's in that raw and gestational state, and that person is in fact in the grip of such unconscious motives...all I can say is, Katie bar the door. Keep your head cool and your wits at hand... you will need them all.

Bad notes take many forms, such as when someone suggests you change something so fundamental, it completely derails the original impulse. ("Why is this a comedy?" "Couldn't the hero be a vampire?" "Does it have to be a Maltese *falcon*?"). Trust me...as notes go, these are the worst. The critic is either proposing the story he'd rather write if he could, or is commenting merely for the sake of commenting. If you work with an agent, be prepared that he or she, a supposed expert on what sells, may hand you a list of such notes to make your work more "commercial."

Sometimes, a person will envy what you've written, so much so that he wants to claim partial authorship by sneaking a bit of his own DNA, as it were, into your baby... sick but true. Or he or she might be trying to sabotage your work and hurt your feelings out of simple competitive spite. Sometimes, he or she may have nothing to say at all, but feels self-conscious and thus compelled to make something up, in order to seem profound. And so on and so on. There's a saying, "When you're twenty, all you care about is what others think of you. When you're forty, you stop caring what others think. And when you're sixty, you realize that nobody was actually thinking of you in the first place." When it comes to your writing, I want you to jump to sixty. Don't assume anyone is actually talking about your work...or that they're looking at it clearly and critically, and are responding to its unique flaws, its singular potential, its essence. Don't ever take their comments (either favorable or negative) personally, but always assume the worst. Beware of others.

The trick, of course, is how to do this while staying open to the good criticism... for there is good criticism out there. It may not be the loudest or the most articulate, it may come from an unlikely source, and it may certainly be the most painful and unpleasant. To hear it properly, you yourself must keep your *own* agenda at bay—and that's perhaps the most difficult challenge of all. Is there a writer who doesn't somehow want to be published, produced, praised and, of course paid? But if you think of your work as the innocent heroine of a Victorian stage melodrama, it is your obligation to figure out who is her true love while rejecting the blandishments of those with baser motives. The stakes are high. Bad criticism can be as poisonous as a bewitched apple delivered by a malefactor, whereas good criticism can unlock the secret door that has hitherto eluded you.

And now that I've given you my big piece of advice—beware of others—let me give you another that may seem at odds with the first. And that is: Find your allies.

By allies, I don't mean friends, although friends are certainly important. I don't even necessarily mean other writers; the novelist Cormac McCarthy, for example, apparently shuns the company of other authors and spends his time socializing with scientists. Writers are hardly strangers to the dark influence of envy, competition and bitterness; just spend some time at certain writers' colonies if you don't believe me. What I mean by allies are people you can trust: people who do not bring an agenda to the table when they hear your work; people who support you without undue judgment in the peculiar and solitary vocation you have chosen called writing; people, in short, who have your back. If you can find allies who are also good critics, then you are doubly blessed. Treat them kindly, invite them over for dinner, and always remember what they drink.

And perhaps that is the final thing with which you leave Goddard: an ally or two, a sympathetic soul who not only shares some of your writerly joys and disappointments, but can serve as a clear-eyed accomplice to your work. If you have been so fortunate as to find a person like that, then your time here will have been more than well spent.

Congratulations again...and please, remember to back up your files.

—*Delivered Summer, 2009, Plainfield, Vermont*

V. Form and Content

FINDING MY RANGE: FORM FOR MY FATHER
By Kyle Bass

"To begin (writing, living) we must have death."
—Hélène Cixous

"We have the right to lie, but not about the heart of the matter."
—Antonin Artaud

When I was thirteen years old I wrote a poem about my father. Three compact stanzas of short lines: my basketball-tall and lean father captured in maybe fifty words. I entered my untitled poem in a poetry contest and it won honorable mention. I would later title my poem about my father "Honorable Mention."

I'm writing a play called *Leeboe & Sons.* I've been working on it for a while now, for too long. I treat my unfinished draft like a canvas: I pull it out, paint on it, cover it again, let it sit. It's not how I usually work on a play. I have Act I and the final scene. The rest is an empty grave, a terrifying void—absence. I fear it might die in my hands.

Leeboe & Sons is about two African American brothers—Clyde, a sick and down-to-his-last-dollar hustler; Dee, a failed boxer turned factory worker—trying to sort out *their* relationship while each tries to come to terms with their father, Manny Leeboe, dead ten years and even more troubling to his sons in death than he was when he was alive.

I write a lot about fathers and I write a lot about death. So perhaps it comes as no surprise when I tell you that my father is dead. The funny thing is that my mother is alive and well, yet for every father alive—in body or in spirit—in my writing, there is a mother undisturbed in her grave. (I suppose I can count Walt Disney as among my earliest influences.)

In the ten years since my father's death, my writing has been haunted by the constant appearances of fathers, father figures, sons, and deaths. After she heard one of my plays read, my grandmother, my father's mother, said, "You stay lookin for your daddy, don't you, baby?" I'm not alone in this. Hardly. I have models: August Wilson's Troy Maxson in *Fences*, a picture of volcanic, hemmed-in rage, shares biographical DNA with Wilson's step-father; Eugene O'Neill's James Tyrone in *Long Day's Journey into Night*, the playwright's washed-up-actor father rendered as a small man still great in his own mind; and *The Late Henry Moss*, another of Sam Shepard's portraits of his father, resurrected as a drunken figure, in the form of a ghost.

I was invited to a playwrights conference hosted by Edward Albee. During a discussion, Albee remarked that he didn't like it very much when people tried to glean facts about his real life, particularly his childhood and his parents, from reading and seeing his plays. *The Goat, or Who is Sylvia?* is Albee's sharp drama about a stylish and intelligent couple, parents to a gay son, whose brittle world is shattered when it's revealed that the husband is in love with a goat named Sylvia, and is in fact having sexual intercourse with Sylvia the goat on a disturbingly regular basis.

A single moment in Albee's play stands out for me. It's when the gay son, Billy, desperate for his father's love and approval, kisses his father... first *on the hands*, Albee tells us in his stage directions, *then on the neck, crying the while. Then it turns and Billy kisses his father full on the mouth—a deep, sobbing, sexual kiss... The father tries to disengage from his son, but the boy moans, holds on. Finally the father shoves his son away, and the son stands there, still sobbing, arms around nothing...* (102). It's a shocking, heartbreaking and inspired moment of theatricality, spectacle, drama, truth. I asked Mr. Albee where that kiss came from. Breaking his own rule about discussing his work in autobiographical terms, he said, "I suppose I wanted a father I could kiss."

This is what drama allows a dramatist to do: to put his deepest desires and wants into action, safely, without actual consequence.

In *An Anatomy of Drama*, Martin Esslin writes:

"Drama is the most concrete form in which art can recreate human situations, human relationships. And this concreteness is derived from the fact that whereas any narrative form of communication will tend to relate events that have happened in the past and are now finished, the concreteness of drama is happening in an eternal present tense, not there and then, but here and now" (18).

My father was an alcoholic. Before that, my father was a high school basketball star. When I was a boy, we had a half-court in our backyard. Sometimes my father, high on vodka, still in the tie he wore to work, would pick up the basketball (he called it "the rock") or seize it from my brother's hands, and he would take shots from the back of the half-court, barking at the ball to "Be there!" When his lazy ball would kiss the rim or brush the bottom of the net—cotton in his day, nylon in mine—my father would say, "Can't find my range," as my brother hurried to retrieve the ball and bounce it back to him, to his ready hands eager to fire again. "Gotta find my range," he'd say and let the next shot go and for a split second his body would be suspended in the air, in the shape of a question mark.

My father never made it easy for himself. He never came in close. He always kept his distance from the rim and moved in a slow arc, adjusting his position against the sun...trying to find his range.

Clyde
There was this one time. Daddy took me out back—when we lived on Park Street—and he pitched to me. Just that one time. I was daddy's little catcher, right? And Daddy, man, he's two sheets to the wind. Cause he's had a nice long talk with that bottle, see, so he's back in that motherfuckin past, right? Throwin that curveball across all them years. Showin me what he's got. Tryin to show me what he can do. What he's capable of. But Manny Leeboe couldn't find it. His shit's high, wide, inside and in the dirt. Daddy was everywhere but over home plate. But I could tell he used to have it. Cause he's still had some of it. A piece of it. His windup was still good—little shaky at the top. And the way he's holdin that ball, Dee. It's dancin in his hand before he throws it. And then his arm moves like a black whip. And that ball is out his hand 'fore he even lets it go. But he's pitchin out of that bottle. Tryin, you know, to be what he never was. And he keeps sayin "Can't find my range." "Got to find my range." Ain't that him? "Got to find my range." Ain't that Daddy, Dee.

Dee
Yeah, that was him.

Clyde
He keeps throwin. Wild. And I keep chasin that motherfuckin ball all over the goddamn yard. I keep tryin to catch that nigger, but I can't...not always. And that JB's in him good now. And he's sayin to me, keeps sayin to me, "You ain't got no eye for a ball, do you, boy?

*You ain't got it in ya, do ya?" Like I'm somebody's fault but not his.
He's drunk and now he's mad. And he's throwin that ball hard, either
from out the past or at it. I can't tell. He's throwin it at me is what it
feels like. "Got to find my range." He keeps sayin that. "Got to find
my range." Throwin like he don't even see me no more. It's getting
dark, Dee. I'm gettin afraid. Cause it's dark to where I can't see him
no more. Can't see where his ball is comin from. Where it's goin. Then
I can't see the ball no more. But I can see that ring on his finger.
Shinin. Like a light far off. So I keep my eye on that cause it's all I can
see. But I hear his voice. I can still hear it! "Got to find my range...
Find my range!"... High and away was as close as he come. . . .*

　　　[Slight pause]
　　　Daddy ever do you like that, Dee?
　　　[Dee shakes his head "no."]

Clyde
Lotta fathers like that out there, huh?

...I'm showing too much of my hand here, I know.

On Thanksgiving afternoon, 1996, my father asked me if I was
still writing. It was small-talk. I told him I was thinking about writing
an autobiographical novel. I was just talking to be talking.

After a moment, my father said, "Will I be in your book?"

"In one form or another," I said.

"Wait until I'm dead," my father told me.

My father had stopped drinking by then.

He lived two more years.

Defeated by cancer, my father died in a hospice in Rochester, New
York. All except my brother gathered there to be with him as he expired.
My 84-year-old grandmother was there at my father's bedside, crying,
calling her 63-year-old son "baby" and asking God to help her let go of
her youngest child, her only son, the second of her three grown children
she and my grandfather would outlive.

My brother, whose relationship with our father had run hot in a
difficult direction, stayed at his home in Los Angeles. When my father
was very near the end, unconscious and drifting from us on a compas-
sionate flow of morphine, we reached my brother by phone to let him

know. What he had to say, if anything, I'll probably never know, but my brother asked that the phone be put to my father's ear. The pale receiver looked like a small baby curled and resting against my father's unconscious, vaguely troubled-looking face. After a moment of silence and stillness, my mother took the phone from my father's ear and said to my brother on the other end, "Okay now?"

* * *

On a windy, bitterly cold but snow-less day in February 2006, in the eighth year of our father's death, my brother flew from Los Angeles to Syracuse, where I live. A cousin of ours—slightly older than me, slightly younger than my brother—had died young and my brother had come home for the funeral. The plan, suggested by our mother, was for me to meet my brother at the airport and together we would make the 30-mile drive to our cousin's funeral.

We were not close, my only brother and I. Between us lay the half-forgiven wounds of a deeply adversarial childhood together and, from earlier in our adult lives, my silent regrets and his swallowed resentments over old un-repaid loans, borrowings lost to the fog and wreckage of substance abuse. And now our relationship was freighted with the unopened, un-shared memories of our dead father. We had a tacit agreement not to talk about Dad.

With time to kill before we headed to the funeral for our cousin, after I collected my brother at the airport I drove him to my home, where he'd never been before. In nearly every room in my house there are pictures of my father—in my office: a picture of my father as a boy, about seven years old, holding a baseball, standing at the front of a group of men, one of them his father; in my bedroom: a picture of my father standing half-naked at the beach where he and my mother first met, twenty-one years old, two years married, his body lean and toned from pick-up games played on hot asphalt; and on the mantle, a picture of my father smiling, his arm around his best friend and drinking buddy, Pete, taken not long before my father learned—or perhaps he knew but hadn't yet told us—that he was sick and going to die.

As I led my brother through my home, showing him where and how I lived, I could see him noticing the pictures of our father, but he did not mention them. "Nice house," my brother said each time we left one of its rooms.

In the kitchen, I asked my brother if he was hungry. He said he was and I made him an omelet and a piece of toast. I asked him if he still liked red jelly with his eggs, as he had when we were growing up, and suddenly he looked and sounded like our father when he said, "That'll work."

I sat at the table with my brother as he ate. We made our small talk: the mundane facts of our grownup lives buoyed by weak jokes, chatter to cover our familiar and accepted ignorance of how to be with each other. I was in my early forties, my brother was nearly fifty, and though I felt a baseline familial love for him, I knew we would never share the kind of brotherly closeness that would have made these very words obsolete. But in a haunted silence that followed my mention of our passed-away cousin, I was soothed by what felt like an understanding between my brother and me: we shared a fear and accepted that this day and the sorrow-tinged journey it held for us would, for a time, bring us as close as we might ever be.

My brother stayed downstairs while I went up to get dressed for the funeral. As I put on my dark suit, I thought about my last moments alone with my father, eight years before—he lay unconscious and ashen in his final bed; I told him I loved him; I kissed my father on his mouth, his faint breath faintly sweet, faintly sour, his still lips the dry edges of life; I told him it was all okay—and my tears came with my hope that my brother, through the phone pressed to our father's ear that day, had found a way to whisper his forgiveness, too.

[Dawn. Dee's apartment. Clyde is at the table. There's a bottle of booze and a glass with three inches of whiskey in it standing before him. He's worn out. Jazz music—at once discordant and harmonious—pours softly from the radio. Dee enters from outside. He sees Clyde at the table but can't see that Clyde has been shot and is bleeding out.]

Dee
You're gonna hurt yourself, drinking like that.

Clyde

Look that way, don't it? C'mon Dee, have one with me. To Manny Leeboe. And sons... Have one with me 'fore I go.

[Dee pauses. Then he gets a glass and brings it to the table. Clyde pours his brother a drink. His hand trembles. Dee starts to help his brother pour.]

I got it. Let me do it.

[Clyde finishes the pour. The brothers drink without ceremony. Long pause.]

Dee

You hungry?

Clyde

Yeah.

[Dee goes to the refrigerator and opens the door.]

Dee

Got two eggs. You want an egg? Before you go?

Clyde

Yeah.

[Dee takes the eggs and some butter to the stove. He strikes a match and lights a burner and puts a pan on the flame. He puts butter in the pan. Clyde takes a drink. It goes down hard. Dee gets two small plates and silverware and sets them on the table. He turns to the stove. His back is to Clyde through the rest of the scene.]

Clyde

Listen, Dee...

Dee

Been thinking about getting back in the gym.

Clyde

Yeah? The ring?

[He coughs. He's bleeding heavily now.]

Dee

No. A trainer. Down to the Y. They got some angry boys down there don't know what to do with their fists.

Clyde

Yeah. You'd be good for that.

[Pause. He takes the wad of cash from his jacket pocket.]
Look, Dee—

[But he can't speak for the pain he's in. He lays the cash on the table in front of Dee's chair.]
Dee, listen—

Dee

[Continuing with the eggs, his back to Clyde.]
What do you want, Clyde?—How do you want your egg, man?

Clyde

[Instead of what he had intended to ask.]
... Break that yolk for me, 'kay?

[Dee breaks the eggs into the pan. Clyde rests his head on his crossed arms. Outside, the city is coming to life, the sound of children running into the street and a father calling after them. Dee watches over the eggs. Clyde is still. The music dies as the lights slowly fade to black.]

Endings, they're hard. They usually come too late, and yet we must not rush toward them.

I thought it would be easier to write about the dead than to write about the living; we can lie about the dead, the living hold us accountable. But another image has come to me: my father—or perhaps it's my brother, father to a son of his own now—standing in a field, waving his arms, calling across the distance. Maybe that's how my play ends...or begins...or begins anew.

—*Delivered Summer, 2008, Plainfield, Vermont*

FORM AND CONTENT
By Rachel Pollack

That which is below is like that which is above
that which is above is like that which is below
to do the miracles of one only thing.

These words are Sir Isaac Newton's translation of the opening of *The Emerald Tablet*, a short deeply layered document written some 1600 years ago, in Alexandria, Egypt. *The Tablet* is the foundation stone for a vast body of work, known as the *Hermetica*, after its supposed creator, a godlike teacher named Hermes Trismegistus. In its two brief pages, it outlines an entire cosmos in which Above—the heavens—and Below—human life—are deeply entwined, mirrors of each other. Through the eyes of Hermeticism, form, the structure of existence, and content, the experiences of our lives, are in fact one and the same. This unity is not static. The text does not say "to be," but "to do the miracles of one only thing." Notice the odd play of plural and singular. There is one thing, the unified cosmos of form, but the miracles are constant, for content continuously reenacts form.

It is worth considering what that form was. From our standpoint on Earth, without a telescope or other aids, it is possible to observe seven heavenly bodies that move with relative speed against the backdrop of the much more slow-moving star constellations. These seven bodies are the Sun, the Moon, Mercury, Venus, Mars, Jupiter, and Saturn, called planets, or "wanderers" by the Greeks. The ancients saw these not simply as objects but as gods, each with its own special quality, and thus a particular influence over human life, both collectively and individually.

From our standpoint here on Earth these wanderers seem to move around us in seven concentric spheres. Because the stars appear so faint, and so slow, people understood that they were outside those spheres. The "planets" moved through the constellations as through a landscape, and the planets/gods acted differently according to the constellation they were visiting. As a soul moved towards incarnation in a body it traveled from the divine realm beyond the planets, through each of the spheres, picking up qualities from each one until it came to the innermost sphere, the Earth (it is a modern fantasy that ancient peoples believed the Earth was flat). When it reached Earth, the soul settled within the particular form of an individual body at the moment of birth. The soul as content, the body as form. This is a mirror of our writing. An idea moves through layers of development, layers of form, until it emerges as a living story, poem, play.

How was the unique content of a human being determined? The planets move against the backdrop, not just of the stars as a whole, but of the constellations. Thus, as your soul passed through the sphere of Venus, goddess of love, whatever constellation Venus was "in" would determine what quality it gave you. For example, if Venus was in Leo, the lion, you might be assertive and confident in love and sexuality. This was the cosmological basis of astrology, known until modern times as the "queen of sciences" for its ability to order all the complex content of our lives into a form that was simultaneously vast and personal.

A remnant of the ancient cosmos, and so a remnant of that bond of form and content, lives on in the seven days of the week. Each one is in fact named for one of the seven planets, and for the supposed influence that planet/god wields over that day. We do not see this readily because in English four of the names—Tuesday to Friday—are based on the Germanic title for that planet and god. Tuesday, for example, is named for Tiw, the German god of war, and thus the planet Mars. Our culture retains vestiges of the seven planetary spheres in other ways, such as the idea that a person reaches maturity at the age of twenty-one, three times seven.

There is something about the number seven. I've been told that if you take a deck of cards and shuffle them seven times they will retain nothing of the original configuration. Not six, not eight, but seven. The ancient mathematician and mystic Pythagoras determined, through experimentation with shortened strings, that the musical scale contains seven natural intervals before returning to the original note at a higher "octave," a word that just means the eighth note. Pythagoras, and later Plato, assumed that each of these seven notes belonged to one of the seven planetary spheres—how could they think otherwise?—so that the movement of the planets would create "the music of the spheres."

When we see the wondrous rainbow across the sky its light breaks into seven colors. Ancient physiology teaches us that there are seven energy centers in the human body. Called *chakras* by the Hindus, these centers follow the seven colors of the rainbow, only in reverse, like a mirror image. That is, red appears at the top of the rainbow but as the "root" chakra, at the bottom of the spine, while violet, the lowest color on the rainbow, shines at the top of the human head, the "crown" chakra.

In the Renaissance, observations of the heavens became more precise, so that it became more and more complicated to maintain the vision of the seven spheres around the Earth. Finally, Copernicus, a deeply religious man and a Hermeticist, restored order to God's cosmos by shifting the Sun to the center of the planetary cosmos, with the Earth now one of the planets orbiting our local star.

This shift made for a more sensible world, but it also broke that unity of Above and Below. Astrology became no longer a science but a kind of divination, that is, a way to form patterns from a set of images. To the Romantics, and the Modernists that came after them, we can no longer see the physical universe as alive, and vital, and connected to our individual lives. The form has broken, and the content becomes fragmented. As we write our literature, and our lives, we do not see them as part of a great unity but rather the struggle of individual expression.

The Romantics, especially Blake, attacked Newton for imposing Reason on the world and thus draining it of life, of what they called the "sublime." But Newton, like Copernicus, was a Hermeticist, a passionate student of alchemy and astrology. The purpose of his great work, *Principia*, was the restoration of unity through the discovery of universal principles that would apply to the heavenly bodies as well as to human life. He achieved this in a mechanical way—the "laws" of gravity apply equally to a human being walking across a room and the planet Venus orbiting the Sun—but not in a spiritual and emotional way.

These are large subjects, and yet they speak directly to our writing, for the form of our world—how we perceive our existence—permeates the content of our work. And vice versa. We begin with experiences, images, ideas, and constantly seek the form to contain them.

Sometimes the content must break old forms, create new ones to express what it needs to say. We see this, for example, in the operas of Richard Wagner, who shocked the musical world when he created new forms to express his musical and mythic ideas. We see it in the massive graphic novel *The Sandman*, in which the writer Neil Gaiman, with various artists, created a new structure, large enough to contain his vision of a universe of stories. We see it in Ralph Waldo Emerson's speech, "The American Scholar," in which he took the conventional form of a commencement address and opened it up with a content so radical for its time that decades later one of those graduating students wrote that anyone who was there never forgot it for the rest of his life.

And we see this creation of new forms in people's lives as well, for we all "write" who we are, and we all seek to find the form to express the content of our truth. I want to talk for a moment about Christine Jorgensen, the original "transsexual," a term coined some years after her famous surgery. Some years ago I hosted an evening in honor of the fortieth anniversary of that surgery. When I considered the question of form and content I remembered that evening, and the stories people told of what Christine Jorgensen had meant to them. And I thought of what she did, the most radical expression of an inner content changing and shaping the literal form of the human body.

It is important to remember that she did not simply change her form to match an inner content, one that already existed but needed expression. Instead she created something entirely new, so that the content itself was born along with the form, the two inseparable, the Emerald Tablet's "miracles of one only thing."

We should not view Christine Jorgensen through the lens of a world she herself created. Like all great artists, whether of literature or the body, she created a form, a path, that others have since followed. At that event I hosted, writer and activist Riki Anne Wilchins said, "We come together to claim our own, our history, and our Christine. Christine, standing alone in God's own light, in a way none of us have had to since, made all of this, and all of us, possible." A great artist creates new forms to give life to new content. Those who follow, such as Riki Anne, or myself, find our own necessary form to discover, and grow, the content of our lives.

Let us return finally to ancient teachings, and the relationship of soul and body. If we consider soul as the content of our writing, and body the form, we may learn something from the ways people have seen that connection.

Most of us in the modern world have only the vaguest idea of soul. If asked, we might describe it as some essence that lives inside the body, almost trapped or held prisoner, liberated only when we die. With such a model we often struggle with the form of our writing, seeing it as a clumsy intractable prison that stifles the content we seek to liberate onto the page.

But there are at least two expressions of form and content that may prove more valuable. The ancient rabbis taught that the soul of a person secretes a body around it. Through biological processes the body grows in the mother's womb, but at the same time a spiritual process is taking place, so that a human being emerges after nine months, a miracle of one only thing. We begin a work of literature with a seed, an idea, a desire. Through the writing that seed of content, the soul of the work, secretes its necessary form around it, an organic unity.

The writer Tom Cowan has described yet another view of the soul. The Desert Fathers of the early Christian Church taught that the soul is in fact larger than the body. It consists of the experiences and under-standings that we have and will have, through the course of our lives. Consider, then, the idea that the true content of your work is in fact larger than the current form you have given it. Through the process of writing the form expands, and the truth of what you write expands as well. This is the constant enactment, the constant doing, of the "miracles of one only thing."

—*Delivered Summer, 2008, Plainfield, Vermont*

TEXT AND SUBTEXT
By Susan Kim

Interior. Restaurant. Evening.

A man walks in and sits at a table. He puts money in the tabletop jukebox; his wife enters. She sits; they chat. Their son enters and they eat onion rings. Other people come in. A man goes to the bathroom. Outside, their daughter finally manages to park her car. She rushes in. Her father looks up. Cut to black. The end.

For a brief, shining moment this month, this country actually cared—deeply—about text and subtext.

Yes, I know...it really, really pissed them off. But at least they were talking about it.

You heard the most unlikely people talking about the final episode of the HBO series *The Sopranos*. It was all over the streets, in the newspapers and on TV, online and at work—people were arguing with anger, conviction, and overwhelming emotion, and all of them, eerily enough, using the language of subtext. Feverishly, they debated symbolism. They discussed dream imagery and religious iconography, recurrent dialogue, filmic references, pop culture allusions. The show's creator, David Chase, actually managed to get people to do what literature professors and writing instructors have been trying—and failing—to do for decades. Not bad for someone who also created the singularly underwhelming *The Rockford Files*.

So how did this great national debate come about? It arose, simply, because people wanted a clear and unambiguous ending for a story they cared about, a dramatic payoff in satisfyingly black and white terms. Whether they had ever even heard of Aristotle, viewers found they desperately craved catharsis through the structure of tragedy. In short, they wanted closure.

And why not? For years, the *text* of *The Sopranos* had been a recognizable, complex tale of power, violence and sex in the Mafia with a little family dysfunction thrown in. Naturally, then, viewers felt sucker-punched by what they felt was an insipid and deliberately, maddeningly ambiguous ending. They felt furious, suspicious, exasperated.

And yet, craving closure, they continued to grapple with that which lay *beneath* the text—the subtext—doggedly hunting down and worrying clues like a game of *Where's Waldo*. What did that cat *mean*, anyway? Or those onion rings? Or that awful song by Journey? Obsessed with puzzling out the *external logic* of that one scene—i.e., was Tony Soprano finally killed or wasn't he?—people chose to ignore the subtext of the entire series itself: which was a Sophoclean story of fate, matrophobic anxiety, self-knowledge, and the elusive nature of transcendence.

In the world of dramatic writing, this is not an especially good time historically for subtext. Perhaps this is symptomatic of a culture that seems increasingly to distrust the inner life as the messy, unruly, and contradictory thing that it is—preferring, for example, to merely *medicate* any bothersome physical or psychological symptoms, without even trying to uncover, much less resolve, the underlying problems or causes.

But I digress.

Today, for better or for worse, drama is overwhelmingly represented by commercial film and television, and Hollywood, as we all know, is run not by the individual artist, but by committees of executives—a true double negative. Thus the stories Hollywood produces are essentially factory-made, and not unlike its human stars: glossy, wafer-thin, unnaturally structured, indistinguishable, and, ultimately, forgettable.

More so than at any other time in its history, Hollywood story structure has been effectively reduced to its barest, most sterile, and least resonant bones, upon which ever greater amounts of money, but few essential changes, are constantly spent. "The protagonist wants, he or she (usually he) pursues, he or she gets." The end. We have been educated to believe that this constitutes not only a happy ending, but in many ways, the *only* ending possible... that life, in effect, exists solely in the two dimensional world of text.

And yet, oddly enough, it was not always this way. Those who disdain any film made before, say, *Dances with Wolves* generally look down on what they assume to be its inaccessible and incomprehensible naiveté, utter lack of sophistication, old-fashioned sentiment, and overall corniness. Yet even the creakiest genre film from the 1930s through the 50s—gangster, Western, horror film, war film—often possessed an unselfconsciousness and exuberant love of the form, not to mention historical and biographical context, that lent it surprising subtextual depth that persists to this day.

The low budgets and rapid production schedules of B-movies generated stories that were unlabored and often ignored by executives, censors, and other professional purveyors of taste and text. Working in such relative freedom—yet with constraints of both time and money—filmmakers often managed to create stories that, like any good dream, shimmered with subtext, whether they intended them to or not.

Watch the noir classic *Gun Crazy* by Joseph Lewis, or any of the old Universal horror films like *The Mummy* or *The Wolf Man*—all of which deliver satisfying genre text while working on profound subtextual levels dealing with sexuality, repression, and duality. Or think of the historical context of films like the 1952 Western *High Noon*. The story of a lone man of principle abandoned by faithless friends takes on completely new meaning when you consider it was made during the height of the Hollywood blacklist. Or rethink any frothy *Broadway Melody* musical or screwball comedy from the 1930s when you contemplate that they were produced during a financial downturn so severe, it literally destabilized the world economy for years. Significance bubbles both beneath and on top of the actual text—infusing the work with meaning far richer than its creators could have ever anticipated.

And yet, scarier than any horror film, the industry changed. It became more than respectable; it became insanely profitable. To this day, entertainment is America's second biggest export right after military equipment. The slow death of the "mid-list" of films, the co-option of independent films by the major studios, and the overreliance on the insanely budgeted blockbuster model means there's very little individualized, creative air in the room any more. As if by corporate fiat, dramatic action over the last thirty years seems to have become uniformly sanitized and externalized, and so is it a surprise that Disney bases some of its most profitable films on its theme park rides?

Subtext is defined as that which is not overtly present in the text, but what of meaning is overtly present in the text of our lives? Life is not neat, but incredibly messy, primarily because people are notoriously unaware of themselves. Dramatic writing may be expressed primarily through dialogue, but it is always driven by action: what people want, what people *think* they want, and what they actually deep down really, *truly* want. When you get right down to it, most people, after all, are unreliable narrators of their own lives, which means by definition, dramatic writing is all about subtext. Talk to any actor, who essentially works in reverse compared to playwrights, in order to accomplish the same thing: to understand the subtext, and to play the action. And that is not just an imitation of life, as Aristotle would have it, it *is* life.

In this way, you can read *A Streetcar Named Desire* not as merely a story of a neurotic woman and her domineering brother-in-law...but as a profoundly political play about power and fragility, written by an openly gay man. Similarly, you can watch *The Chairs* and appreciate it as Eugene Ionesco's response to World War II, which anchors the absurdism and makes it an extraordinarily moving theatrical experience. In an essay by Wilfred Sheed, *Harold Pinter's Birthday Party* is presented as not merely an allegory of the artist as hapless victim of society, but as thinly-veiled autobiography, with its roots in his unhappy childhood as an outsider in the British countryside. And so it goes with every great piece of dramatic literature ever written.

Ultimately, drama, whether on screen or onstage is like all art—timelessly vital because it is interactive, and interactive because it demands engagement. It doesn't merely seek to manipulate an emotional response to text; instead, it uses its own tools of symbolism, humor, allusion, and context to spark associations, raise questions, and trigger emotional and intellectual investment. All it requires is that you bring your own life experience, knowledge, and an open mind to engage in the dialogue. For after all, subtext is the ghost in the machine, the spirit that ultimately animates the text.

—*Delivered Summer, 2007, Plainfield, Vermont*

WOULD I LAND

By Douglas A. Martin

I first wrote for my mother, truly, something to show her. She was off at work, and she'd be home in another half hour or so, right after school let out, and my sister and I had walked, house key safety-pinned inside the pocket of my pants, blocks home: four or five only, but our legs were shorter then, so the distance, that perspective, stretches, time elongates: a long, long walk of ten, fifteen minutes.

With such stretches now, I'm just getting warmed up. The writer walks: mad Swiss Robert Walser, melancholic German-writing Sebald, the visionary prodigy that Rimbaud is before Rimbaud folded his hands on his poetry, shut his eyes to the sighs and signs inside and opted rather for the gun trade and more and more gold amassed, in a most horde-able, tangible, form from far-flung outposts.

Still we send letters.

In the form of one, Virginia Woolf addresses walking too, in her anti-war, anti-patriarchal, anti-fascist late text *Three Guineas*: "Three years is a long time to leave a letter unanswered, and your letter has been lying without an answer even longer than that. I had hoped it would answer itself, or that other people would answer it for me. But there it is with its question…"

The question is how to prevent war, still unanswered.

Skeptical of the pomp and circumstances of such occasions as costumed graduations, the military, popes, marching bands, the boy scouts, doctors filing out along a lawn, caps and robes and gowns all a flutter, all the part of some same hooding system regulating, regimenting, so forcefully, Woolf's oblique argument in conception is illustrated through black-and-white accompanying pictures of these such parades, pageantry, pictures later in turn suppressed as would be part of her then apparent argument: as these photos are removed from later editions of the text, meaning circulates then more a blank.

I'm not an historian, and neither does Woolf's narrator have to be to make her connections. She just had to know where to look.

I'd say we are already one step in the right direction, here, today.

Left, right.

I'd say listen to the fact that many voices will be heard here, as many voices as pairs of feet—Tom and Jerry as we called 'em as kids—coming up to receive, many more here than just me. A chorus I'm honored to add myself to as just one element.

Among other things, Virginia Woolf pondered the placing of the "PhD" after a name, insisting one's worth be recognized there in that. (That might be in, or also in, *A Room of One's Own*.)

To give you an illustration of my own priorities, I did not walk for my BA (English), though I did make sure to plan to ask my mother up to New York, when I moved far away there, for her to come see me come up to get a daisy as part of my very own MFA graduation. To come up to the church on 5th Ave. used for other things, and to sit there next to me.

She tells me how for her second wedding she was not allowed to wear white, how you only got to do that the first time. It was one day I remembered as about me in some way, but not really only. My sister and I stood to the side, where we watched proceedings.

Once—I was still even younger, less skeptical of my own impressionability—I took a spiral outside under a tree and began there in a notebook putting two things together, one form, one medium, to form another. I'd taken four characters from *The Guiding Light*—off the air now—my mother used to pick us up from the nursery in time hopefully to catch the last thirty minutes of it, before we could do that walking home from the school ourselves. I think I was in the third grade. These teenagers called themselves the Four Musketeers; I put them into the Nancy Drew formula. I was this postmodernist before I even knew such words to claim for a condition, any possible theoretical validity to my hybrid instincts, my endeavors, *real* reactionary import to the impetus of some sympathies. I was going to start my book that afternoon, and add more to it in the evening, so my mother could read it when she got home from work.

I would be the only one in my immediate family to go to college, and more college, and more.

From my lows to my highs. In a book, one could dwell in a different landscape. In a book, occasionally, there would be flashes of what I could be. And no, if you asked me I'd say I didn't believe there was any man up there, though some nights far from home, all I'd so horribly known, in New York when I felt so alone I couldn't sleep, that entity of her up there I looked up to—a round, quiet, solidness, a calming bit of something greater than all of us, so self-assured, so self-selecting—the moon.

The tree I wrote against was a pine—not the magnolia I'd earlier tried flying off from, jumped and fell; my pining now, my crow-cawing, every time pen hits paper.

Lest I get too far away from my shores, I turn back to American Gertrude Stein, who proposes: "One cannot come back too often to the question what is knowledge and the answer knowledge is what one knows." That is from her essay "What Is English Literature." English Literature is like an island, she goes on to formulate. And, "It is awfully important to know what is and what is not your business. I know that one of the most profoundly exciting moments in my life was when at about sixteen I suddenly concluded that I would not make all knowledge my province."

To start the first class of each semester I studied with her pursuing my most advanced degree, foundational queer theorist and my late professor, Eve Kosofsky Sedgwick would say, inviting us too to imagine what we really might be more like inside, "My name is Eve and I'm a panda." We'd go then around the room, all naming our own selves, our own animals identifying, though these IDs could be with the inanimate, too, of course.

A degree is a matter of how much you've committed yourself within certain perimeters. I think I've found a most perfect thing to say. I'm pondering on this while walking the woods with Darcey, also one of my teachers and friends, Abbie, her daughter and friend.

An invitation to speak is a letter that has not been answered until the speaker concludes and takes a seat. I am looking for a precision that might be also open, welcoming, inviting, I hope. I am striking here against tendencies to make some overarching statements. Reflects auteur Robert Bresson: "It is from being constrained to a mechanical regularity, it is from a mechanism that emotion will be born. To understand this, think of great pianists." Or, if you wish, you with your envelopes, the alphabet, your languages. Writing is this thing: the more you need it, the more it can be there for you, the more you can always call upon it. It can create the space or it can take up the slack. It can be a compacting of the negatives into new starting points. Writing is our offering, what offers itself up to be constantly renewed. You could strive to make it thicker, richer, more well wrought, finely filigreed or solidly constructed, always going back over these designs.

Much might come home to roost, then, in communication.

We writers are animals of many different stripes. We forge on. We camp out. In small movements or grand gestures, in quiet murmurs or sweeping scales.

Whatever other trappings it brings, here is this thing we have that the other animals don't, so far as we can tell: call it secondary symbolization if you want to get fancy. Rimbaud, in his precocious, shifting menagerie of imagery, in *Vowels*, his promising poem from the 1870s, begins by assigning color-codes: "Black A, White E, Red I, Green U, Blue O: vowels/I will one day speak your hidden mysteries." He then begins to wind up: "The peace of pastures dotted with animals, the peace of the furrows which alchemy prints on broad studious foreheads."

You learn when you learn you can let yourself. You can know more through the conversing you embark upon. Many roads lead here, and many roads lead back out.

Many roads lead the way onward. I hope you've all found some little help down the best path. Each of you, in your own ways, in pages, sentences, dialogues, lines, have worked to enlarge upon those horizons of perception you first entered upon.

One of our desires as a species is to share, I believe. We contribute what we can. I am happy to stand here on this next brink with you, today. I think I will let myself be quiet now some and give you each time to point to those voices grown.

—*Delivered Summer, 2007, Plainfield, Vermont*

VI. Points of View

DOES A PLANET HAVE A POINT OF VIEW?
By Jan Clausen

When we speak of "points of view," we usually think spatially: about geographic location, social positioning, or psychological perspective. I'm going to take a different tack and ask you to consider point of view as a function of positioning in time: species time, planetary time, location in history.

More specifically, I'm concerned with the problem of what writer Tom Engelhardt refers to as our crisis of "futurelessness." What does it mean for us as writers to be living in a time when we can have no confident assurance that future generations will be around to read our words?

This is obviously a huge question—so huge that it seems not only staggering to confront but almost embarrassing to pose. I often feel that, like the prospect of our individual deaths, it's something most people have decided ought not to be brought up in polite society. Not that this prohibition has prevented my obsessing about the problem ever since my early childhood, which was spent under the Cold War cloud of nuclear terror, with air raid drills, the fallout shelter craze, and the Cuban Missile Crisis. In those years, concern about the future of human life on earth seemed inevitably linked to the dangers of nuclear weapons. Some of that anxiety went underground with the end of the Cold War and the fond notion that the nuclear standoff had been resolved. It went underground but it didn't go away. And for the past few years we've had our attention re-focused on a range of apocalyptic perils: not only the nuclear weapons that keep on proliferating, but the cumulative collapse of our ever more degraded environment under the joint impacts of high-tech wars, rapacious resource extraction, and worsening global poverty. (Need I mention global warming and emergent epidemics?) A couple of weeks ago, the astrophysicist Stephen Hawking made headlines by calling for humans to colonize space, with the idea that such a move represents the only reliable method for insuring the survival of our species.

As a practical matter, I agree with Alice Walker, who in the early 1980's gave a wonderful, pithy address to an anti-nuclear rally, the text of which was published in *Homegirls: A Black Feminist Anthology* under the title "Only Justice Can Stop a Curse." Walker makes the point that looking to outer space as a safety valve for humanity's destructive behavior on this planet is just an open invitation to extend racist colonialism and exploitative patriarchy to the stars, and the stars don't deserve it. So I take a dim view of Hawking's proposed solution, but I do think it's crucial to pose the question head on: where are we, *really*, in human history? How much time do we have? What can be done to better the prognosis? We can all see now, as most of us couldn't years ago during the Cold War, that the real threat is not linked to any specific technology. The ultimate Inconvenient Truth is that a species which evidently lacks an efficient survival instinct (and may in fact be argued to possess a potent death wish) has got its hands on a range of methods for committing collective suicide.

In my life as a citizen, I'm very concerned with the political tasks implied by this situation: using the framework supplied by Alice Walker, how can we create the planetary Justice that will stop the Curse of our tremendous destructive capacity? But in speaking to you here at the MFA residency, and in my own creative life, I'm centrally concerned with different tasks—those of the imagination. Learning to live with—let's say to manage—our species' suicidal bent is not only a political assignment but a job for the imagination. We do not really know yet what it means to say that we have brought upon ourselves this Curse of potential and looming self-destruction because it cannot be comprehended as an arrangement of facts, but only as an imagined reality. (I take that phrase from Philip Gourevitch, who writes in his book about the Rwandan genocide, *We Wish to Inform You That Tomorrow We Will be Killed with Our Families*, that when he came to write about Rwanda, he found himself confronted with the seeming paradox of having to imagine through his writing what he already knew to be real.) Likewise, we can't hope to create forms of sane and life-cherishing life—the Justice that stops a Curse—without first imagining their outlines. So we writers have our work cut out for us.

I'm now going to explore these ideas in relation to a couple of writers who mean a lot to me, then draw a connection to my own recent fiction.

It would be well worth the while of anyone who wants to explore this question of historical location as point of view to closely examine the amazing manipulations of perspective that Walt Whitman accomplishes in *Crossing Brooklyn Ferry*. That poem begins, "Flood-tide below me! I see you face to face!/Clouds of the west—sun there half an hour high—I see you also face to face" (189). So it opens in the very immediate present, establishing a relationship with the pulse of the planet itself. Very shortly, however, the speaker reaches forward, expanding the temporal space of the poem to engage in dialogue with future generations, then stepping rhetorically into future space so that we look back on the ancestor-poet in his own time. As in so much of his work, Whitman aims here for what we might call a radically democratic point of view:

Crowds of men and women attired in the usual costumes, how curious you are to me!

On the ferry-boats the hundreds and hundreds that cross, returning home, are more curious to me than you suppose,

And you that shall cross from shore to shore years hence are more to me, and more in my meditations, than you might suppose...

What is it then between us?

What is the count of the scores or hundreds of years between us?

Whatever it is, it avails not—distance avails not, and place avails not,

I too lived, Brooklyn of ample hills was mine,

I too walk'd the streets of Manhattan island...

Wonderfully moving as I find the poem to be, I've also long felt exasperated with Whitman for feeling authorized to write it. My indignation, I've finally realized, has to do with the humanistic smugness, the sheer complacency of his relationship to time. He thought he could count on "generations and generations." I—we—don't have that luxury.

In Muriel Rukeyser's *The Speed of Darkness*, there's a wonderful poem entitled, simply, "Poem." It begins like this:

I lived in the first century of world wars.
Most mornings I would be more or less insane,
The newspapers would arrive with their careless stories...

There's an echo of Whitman in the way that Rukeyser manages to bridge the experience of centuries, and also in the eerie rhetorical stance of posthumous survey. But for Rukeyser, it is the active response to "these wars" that becomes the occasion for connecting:

Slowly I would get to pen and paper,
Make my poems for others unseen and unborn.
In the day I would be reminded of those men and women
Brave, setting up signals across vast distances...

Thus the poem acknowledges that we have entered a fundamentally new situation; in the first "century of world wars" and the similar ones to follow, survival means doing the imaginative work of survival: "to construct peace," to consider "a nameless way of living, of almost unimagined values," to "reach beyond ourselves,/To let go the means, to wake."

Leslie Marmon Silko's novel *Ceremony*, published in the late 1970's, tells the story of Tayo, a young American Indian man who returns to Laguna Pueblo in a shattered state following service in World War II. The novel is about his healing process, but, rather than focusing on individual psychology as one might expect in a novel about post-traumatic stress disorder, *Ceremony* frames Tayo's story in a sacred and mythic dimension of oral narrative, incorporating creation stories and other "time immemorial stories" from Laguna and Navajo tradition. The novel is really about the same thing as Rukeyser's poem: how to use the imagination as a resource to construct survival in the face of humanity's enormous penchant for destruction. Drawing on the imagined reality of her Native American past, in which genocidal assaults on human beings intertwined (and still do) with violence to the natural world, Silko tightly connects war, environmental disaster, racism, and nuclear peril.

Ceremony's approach to framing a protagonist inside mythic narratives allows Silko to touch on the imagined reality of a single fate for the entire human species without committing the artistic and historical sins of a false universalism. Tayo's story of sickness and healing can comment on our collective peril precisely because it is imagined as specific to a particular character, a particular and beloved physical setting, and the particular imagery and rhythms of Laguna Pueblo and Navajo sacred texts. The novel's temporal dimension is similarly multi-layered, simultaneously located in a determinate historical time and in what we might call the "universal time" of myth. This latter is the time in which —so long as human beings take the trouble to follow the Laguna elders' injunction to "remember the story"—past, present, and future may be experienced as existing simultaneously.

I recently completed a novel called *The Company of Cannibals* in which I was finally able to take on, as a creative "object," my lifelong concern with futurelessness. The novel features a group of people who are obsessed with the fate of the earth. At their center is Paula Schweike, a poet turned secular prophet who gives public performances in which she burns her own journals. Paula's disciples face a terrible choice when, in protest against the seemingly terminal condition of the planet, she commits suicide, instructing her nearest and dearest to ingest her remains. In order to tell this story, I found it necessary to construct my own version of the temporal shifts that become point of view shifts in the works I've been discussing here. So we get versions of Paula's tale in the pedantic, chilly voice of a historian looking back from a distance of hundreds of years in the future; in the mythic voice of a quasi-scriptural retelling; in the vernacular voice of collective retrospect; and in the form of documents, including journals, composed by disciples who share in Paula's oddball passion. I found that I had to construct some version of a planetary future—even though one very partially, disjointedly glimpsed—to make the peril of our own present seem sufficiently real. Paula's methods may be questionable but her concern cannot be argued with because the novel gives us the voice of a Redactor telling us that there really was a Universal Crash, which humanity just barely survived. At the same time, constructing an imagined future—however grim—let me, the author, out of the supermax prison of "presentist" thinking in which we all live at least part of the time. It freed me from the cultural tyranny that Guy Debord diagnosed in *The Society of the Spectacle*, whereby only that which "appears" is deemed to have substance or worth.

I want to leave you with a couple of broad ideas and one question. The first idea is that past, present, and future are completely interdependent. Despite our ceaseless efforts to the contrary—our attempts to get closure, to focus on now, to avoid borrowing trouble, and so on and so forth—they simply can't be de-linked. To lose the future is to lose the past, and once that happens, we're standing on a dangerously thin, ultimately untenable and even illusory slice of present time. It follows that we as writers face the crucial task of reweaving the imaginative links between past, present, and future.

The second idea is that there's something in our vocation *as writers* that requires the reasonably secure prospect of a future audience. Very few of us, I believe—even those rare few who enjoy the sort of celebrity for their writing that usually accrues only to stars of more popular media—write *solely* for the present. So much of our odd trade is by way of putting messages in bottles. If we lose confidence that someone will be out there to retrieve them, we might as well pack it in right now.

Finally, and it's far too big a subject to do justice to today, I want to acknowledge that the imagination cannot be commanded. One can't productively sit down and *determine* to write a book that will make a difference to the future of the world. And yet I want to reaffirm that writers have a *collective* responsibility to confront the world with its very real jeopardy, and a corollary obligation to search for and reflect the so far "unimagined values" that might help us keep on keeping on.

The question I'll leave you with is the title of these remarks, and it's sort of a Zen riddle: Does a planet have a point of view?

—*Delivered Summer, 2006, Plainfield, Vermont*

SOME SHORT THOUGHTS ON POINT OF VIEW
VIA THREE POEMS
By Juliana Spahr

I confess, this is the third draft of this talk on point of view.

Part of my inability to write this talk is that point of view is more a device associated with fiction than with poetry. It isn't that poems don't have points of view, but they don't necessarily have to have points of view. And often they avoid them. Or their views are without points. So that is what this talk is about. I've taken three poems to tell three or so poetry-specific things about point of view.

1. When poetry started off a long, long time ago, it was an oral form. And it was collectively written. One could say there is a point of view to things like chants, the point of view of a culture maybe. But that really isn't what we are talking about when we talk about point of view most of the time. Most of the time we mean something specific about the narrator or the voice of a piece of writing.

Literacy changes poetry. And perhaps one could say that point of view arose with literacy? Or maybe what happens is that the possibility of writing being a genre of individualism happens with literacy and the idea that literature can convey individual and specific thoughts is necessary for literature to have a point of view. We start this story of the rise of the individual perspective in poetry in the west usually with Sappho.

Lyric poetry might be the poetry that engages point of view in the most obvious ways as the lover addresses the beloved. In most instances, it is clear who is speaking and who they are speaking to. I should also confess that one of my earlier drafts was a play with this somewhat bad pun between point of view and point of you. I'm easily bothered by the "you" in poetry and see it as one of the most troubled of poetic addresses. I'm easily annoyed by the love poem. I'm easily annoyed by how often it naturalizes the lover and the beloved as a heterosexual couple. By which I mean that I often find its point of view annoying and exclusive. There is, however, no historical justification for my annoyance because Sappho's poetry, what we know of it, might be exemplary for its complicated point of view. In the poem that Mary Barnard translates as "He is more than a hero," the feedback loop of the love poem between the lover and the beloved is fractured as the lover looks at a beloved and the beloved's lover.

2. Skipping way ahead, it is modernism, a form that has closer ties to oral poetries than many acknowledge, that challenges our ability to say anything easy about point of view in poetry. I think the classic example here is Gertrude Stein's work. In *Tender Buttons* she writes a series of poems that are given titles that are often, but not exclusively, objects that one might find in some domestic space. Consider this passage...

DIRT AND NOT COPPER.

Dirt and not copper makes a color darker. It makes the shape so heavy and makes no melody harder.

It makes mercy and relaxation and even a strength to spread a table fuller. There are more places not empty. They see cover.

NOTHING ELEGANT.

A charm a single charm is doubtful. If the red is rose and there is a gate surrounding it, if inside is let in and there places change then certainly something is upright. It is earnest.

MILDRED'S UMBRELLA.

A cause and no curve, a cause and loud enough, a cause and extra a loud clash and an extra wagon, a sign of extra, a sac a small sac and an established color and cunning, a slender grey and no ribbon, this means a loss a great loss a restitution.

With *Tender Buttons*, it is possible to say everything or nothing about point of view. By which I mean one can talk endlessly about whether the poems are written from the point of view of Stein, a middle class woman sitting in a middle class room in France around 1911, or whether they are written from the view of something like Mildred's umbrella (is a sort of giving voice to the umbrella going on?), or some other point of view. There is no clear pronoun use, one of the big point of view clues. There is also no clear perspective, no clear narrator.

As a result, *Tender Buttons* has been relentlessly and at moments wonderfully over-read. Everyone has said almost everything. Bob Perelman sees the work of Stein as "continually at the service of the most ambitious attempts at totalization and social authority" while Marianne DeKoven argues that it is revolutionary, or as she writes "intentionally subversive." While William Gass hears sexual play in *Tender Buttons*, it is all puns about dildos and stuff, and Lisa Ruddick hears religious gnosticism.

Just as Sappho's turn to interiority probably would not have been possible without her having some sort of relationship to literacy, although what sort we don't really know, the lack of a clear point of view of modernism is also shaped by the language politics of the time. When Stein was in Paris writing in *Tender Buttons* "act as if there is no use in a centre," Paris was an imperial center with all the attendant complications that brought to French national culture. 600,000 troops and 200,000 workers were brought into France from the colonies during World War I. European immigration to urban areas such as Paris was also very high at the time. Both these immigrations changed the way the street sounded when one walked down it as all these people brought their languages into the city. This inevitably changed literary practices. Language, the tool that writers use, went from being mono to poly, went from being transparent to unavoidably exposed as shaped by relations between geographically diverse locations. The street we might say had no clear point of view.

So I read Stein less as apolitically avoiding point of view and more suggesting that the singular point of view isn't making any sense any more. That something more webby and tentacled might be needed.

3. After modernism, one among many of the formal devices that become fashionable in US poetries of the last half of the twentieth century are variations on this polyphonic poem with multiple and unlocatable points of view of Stein. It gets used by poets of several different persuasions. Many of the New American Poets, or the poets emerging in the 50s and 60s, use it. And the language poets, emerging in the 70s, both champion it and theorize it.

Although one of the classic modernist examples of the fragmented and ambiguous point of view is Pound's *Cantos* with its fascist ties, many of the poets who use this form argue that there is an almost intrinsic leftist politics to this sort of writing. By the time of this contemporary moment, it is almost as if the poem with the wavering and ambiguous point of view has become a short hand for leftist critique in North American poetry circles. I imagine this looks peculiar to those outside of North American poetry circles. And it might even look weird to some inside various North American poetry circles. There are different versions of this argument. One version concentrates on lyric or on what sometimes got called "expressive centered persona writing" in the 1980s, which is associated with individualism in the bad way. Or in another argument, made by Ron Silliman, clear coherent speech is the tool of the government, the government that was bombing Vietnam, and so one had to fracture it, to break it down, to prevent it from lying and attempting to persuade one to go to war. I confess I'm doing a caricature of a complicated argument and so please realize that these arguments are more complicated than the version I am giving you here.

All of this—that the poem without a fractured point of view is a poem of leftist critique by default—got interestingly tested in the recent debate about Michael Magee's poem *Their Guys, Their Asian Glittering Guys, Are Gay*. The poem goes like this:

Ten years and this will be just another big Asian city, like
countries and let the Empire swallow them for their own benefit.
Brutus and Ajo look at me, pity in their eyes. Maybe the thin
Asian chick, burgundy car coat, Hong Kong chic.

And it goes on to do little more than use the word Asian a bunch more times, often associating the word with a slightly insane stereotype such as "but most Asian people I HAVE MET, are pretty short," or "They like opium," and at other moments just using it descriptively such as, "Asian Santa is 7″ tall."

One thing you need to know about this poem is that it is flarf. Flarf is a form of writing that happens mainly out of New York City sometime after 9/11. In many instances, poems that get called flarf are written by entering a search term into Google or other search engine and then the author edits the poem out of the language that the search engine returns. Flarf is, thus, a variation on the many forms of found poetry that happened in the 60s and 70s, and it is an interestingly pointed development in the fractured language poem written by someone like Bruce Andrews. What comes out, as you might expect, is a fairly wide range of various language habits or patterns. Those who write flarf often exaggerate the sort of uncensored, or what they have called the anti-PC quality, by entering in, shall we say, deliberately unusual or unpoetic terms.

This poem was read in the living room of a small house in Oakland in May of this year. About twenty people were present. After this poem was read, one of those big debates that only happen in small poetry communities in the age of the internet erupted. It happened mainly on three or four blogs. It might have started with Maggie Zurowski's post recalling the reading on her blog, Minor American Poet. And it continued mainly on Kasey Mohammad's Lime Tree and Timothy Yu's Tympan. The debate was provocative, raging, overly simple, dramatically complicated, emotional, rational...all those things debates about literature can be. I'm not going to summarize it; it would take too long. But a huge part of the debate was about the ambiguous and/or multiple points of view in the poem. Magee's argument was that the poem relies on the willingness of readers to read it "as something OTHER THAN autobiographical lyric poems." Or, to put this back into the frame of this talk, as other than a poem with a singular point of view.

Magee in one of his many posts in this debate calls this "occult instability." Or Kasey Mohammad puts it this way:

"Mike's poem isn't saying, 'here, Asian-Americans, let me speak for you,' any more than it is mocking them. It does not represent an occupation of an Asian-American subject position in any way. Nor does it represent an occupation of an *anti*-Asian-American subject position. It is, to my mind, an acknowledgment of the air we *all* breathe—that is the language we speak, think, and are spoken and thought by on a daily basis through little or no choice of our own. It says, 'Yipes, my open mind is full of all this crap that text keeps transmitting!' It says, 'Yipes, all this crap is a constant physical fact of culture that can be ignored only through me pretending I don't see it!' It says, 'Yipes, the only thing I can do with this crap to avoid either internalizing it or letting it make me go crazy is to make a poem out of it!'"

Magee's and Mohammad's argument is somewhat assuming that as readers we can float above the language of a poem and not be caught by it, that a poem with variable points of view allows us to do this. And one of the arguments made by Magee's detractors was that we could not. Tim Yu talks of a "visceral reaction" that the poem cultivates in readers and what I think he might mean by this is that the poem can't escape having a point of view in the reader. He continues: "although it [the lack of a coherent subject position or point of view] may in some sense insulate the poem from a charge that it is coherently 'racist' (in the sense of proceeding from a 'racist' speaker), it also prevents anyone from coherently claiming that the poem is somehow 'anti-racist' (proceeding from a speaker who is clearly opposed to racism). In any conventional sense, then, the poem is *at best neutral* toward its racist material, since it has denied itself the luxury of ironic distance?"

4. I am deliberately avoiding my own point of view on this poem and on flarf in general. I'm not sure I've sorted it out yet, to be honest, but I'm leaning more on the Yu side just because if a poem provokes such debate among like minded readers, I do think that the poem is at best not doing what Magee wants it to do. I felt after this debate that there were still big issues around poetry's forms and politics that are yet to be worked out. The Magee debate is interestingly a debate about craft conventions and how they intersect with identity categories. And I had that feeling that I often have that all the time that is spent in writing workshops about how to turn a metaphor or where to put that comma is missing some of the more resonant debates about how writing critiques supports or tears down or holds up or avoids the problematic language

practices of our times. And while I'm not sure I would want consensus on this debate, I did find the debate about the Magee poem the most interesting when it delved into issues such as whether there was a different valence of critique in something like Bruce Andrews's work (which doesn't dwell on a certain singular identity category) and Magee's poem which concentrates only on the term "Asian."

Actually, I don't have much of a conclusion, so I'm just going to stop. Can I argue that this is a brief history of some poems with point of view issues?

—*Delivered Summer, 2006, Port Townsend, Washington*

LOOKING IN THE JONATHAN MIRROR

By Deborah Brevoort

Last year I became a student again. After teaching for nearly fifteen years, it was refreshing to change my point of view and be in the classroom instead of in front of it. Lynn Thomson, a well-known dramaturg in the professional theatre, assembled a handful of playwrights to get together to study early American theatre, comedy, and music under the auspices of her newly formed theatre group America-in-Play. Experts were brought in once a month to present us with materials and give us writing assignments. Our charge was to use these materials to inspire and create new works for the stage.

Why early Americana? Several years before, Lynn, a PhD candidate in theatre history, had been searching for a dissertation topic. She was in the basement of NYU's Bobst Library when she found a box of unknown American comedies from the nineteenth and early twentieth centuries. Lynn realized that she held in her hands an American folk drama that had been completely lost to historians and theatre practitioners. Not only was her dissertation problem solved, but the next chapter of her professional life in the theatre had begun. Our class was the first page in that chapter.

The plays that Lynn rescued that day contained two features that she recognized from *The Contrast* by Royall Tyler, the first known play written by an American in the 1700's after the Revolutionary War. The first feature was a character named Jonathan—a rough, uneducated fellow from the backwoods of America. The second was a story that centered on Jonathan's adventures in New York City where he encounters refined, educated, aristocratic English types. Thomson writes:

> "I soon realized what scholars would reify, that the characters and stories found within these comedies were larger than any one individual play. Unlike contemporary plays, which pride themselves on originality of story and character, there was an intentional reiteration in the stories and characters of this early canon."

So who was this Jonathan fellow? What did he do? And why did he appear in so many early American plays?

According to Constance Rourke in *American Humor: a Study of National Character*, Jonathan was often a peddler or traveling salesman who was pushing into new territories. He was successful at selling things, so much so that villages would bolt their doors when word arrived that he was coming into town. But Jonathan was so persuasive and charming that the bolted doors would fly open and all the silver in the town would leap into his pockets as soon as he arrived. He was smart, practical, and innovative. He was rough-hewn and uncouth— rural to the core. He was also unschooled and full of bravado.

Jonathan was always shown in opposition to the English, who were portrayed as foppish, silly and insincere. His native American intelligence was shown to be better than the educated British kind, and when unschooled Jonathan was pitted against an over-educated English aristocrat, Jonathan always outsmarted him.

What is significant about Jonathan is that he was the first American character to be created on the American stage. He appeared at a time in our history when the American identity was being formed and when Americans were attempting to define who we were as a nation and a people.

As time went on, and the Jonathan character evolved, the "American vs. the English" dynamic in these stories became the "rural folks vs. the city folks." Bostonians replaced the English. Later still, New Yorkers replaced Bostonians, and the backwoods Jonathan eventually became the middle-American whose native intelligence was considered better than the cultural elite's.

For me, what is most exciting about Jonathan is that he was first created by playwrights. He was born in the theatre and quickly leapt off the stage and entered the culture to become a staple of American humor and the subject of cartoons, songs, political essays, and editorials, according to Rourke. Early America embraced him. In the end, he was a character made by many hands. Each region fashioned him in their own image. There are Vermont Jonathans, Southern Jonathans and

Kentucky Jonathans. Rourke notes that he character was informed by many cultures, as well: Irish, German, French, Hungarian, Spanish, African and Persian influences can be found in his character construct. He later morphed into Yankee Doodle, and then he morphed again into Uncle Sam. The pictures we see today on the "Uncle Sam Wants You" posters are Jonathan.

In Jonathan we find the beginnings of the American distrust of intellectuals, a dynamic that played out in recent presidential elections. The Blue State/Red State divide can be understood by looking at the Jonathan stories. George W. Bush is a modern day Jonathan; he is the embodiment of this national self-portrait. He used it with great success in both of his presidential bids by characterizing himself as the folksy common man pitted against overly educated out-of-touch intellectuals like Al Gore and John Kerry. Jonathan, it turns out, is still very much alive in our culture, even if most people are not consciously aware of him.

I realized that Jonathan was alive and well in me, too. When reading the Jonathan stories, I felt like I was looking into a mirror. I discovered that I had adopted the Jonathan personae—without even realizing it—when I was the Producing Director of Perseverance Theatre in Alaska in the 1980's. It was my job to raise money for the theatre. I would call the foundations in New York City and adopt a folksy way of talking that always got me put through to the head person. When I came to New York I would dress the part, tromping into their offices wearing Alaskan boots and a parka. Once there, I would regale them with exotic tall tales of theatre on the frontier. As with Jonathan, their silver leapt into my pockets. One time I returned to Alaska with $750,000 for Perseverance Theatre. At the time I thought I was simply doing what every Alaskan does when they meet someone from the lower 48: prey on their ignorance of Alaska, exploit their fascination with it and play up my own exotic qualities. Little did I know that this time-honored Alaskan sport was reenacting an old story that was born on the American stage in the 1700's.

Not only did Jonathan give me a new perspective about myself, but studying the early American theatre that he came out of gave me some new insights about contemporary theatre. I was inspired by the fact that the theatre and playwrights played a central and ongoing role in creating and developing our national identity. Up until the 1920's everyone from every segment of society, educated and uneducated alike, attended theatre on a regular basis. In *Highbrow, Lowbrow: the Emergence of Cultural Hierarchy in America*, Lawrence Levine writes that at any given performance you would find "young, old, rich, poor, masters, servants, papists, puritans, church men, statesmen, apprentices, poor workingmen, Negroes and prostitutes." The theatre housed under one roof a microcosm of American society. This was true not only in the cities but on the American frontier as well. The theatre, along with the church, was the center of community life. It was a truly populist activity.

So, what was this early American theatre like? It was an unruly activity both on stage and off. As Levine recounts, "The upper galleries reeked of onions and whiskey, and the crackling of nuts and the crunching of apples saluted my ears on every side." If the American audience didn't like an actor or a performance, they would hiss and stomp their feet. One British observer noted that "the egg as a form of dramatic criticism came into use in this continent." At one performance of *Richard III* in California, the audience was so displeased with the actor portraying Richard that the *Sacramento Daily Union* reported:

" 'Cabbages, carrots, pumpkins, potatoes, a wreath of veg-
etables, a sack of flour and one of soot, and a dead goose, with
other articles, simultaneously fell upon the stage'...The barrage
woke the dead Henry, who fled followed by Richard, his head
'enveloped in a halo of vegetable glory.' Pleas from the manager
induced the audience to allow the play to go on, but not for long.
In act II, McDermott's (the actor playing Richard) inept wooing
of Lady Anne again exhausted the patience of the audience.
'When Richard placed the sword in her hand,' a reporter
observed, 'one half the house, at least, asked that it might be
plunged into his body.' This storm of shouts was followed by

a renewal of the vegetable shower accompanied this time by Chinese firecrackers. As poor Richard fled for the second time, 'a well directed pumpkin caused him to stagger, and with still truer aim, a potato relieved him of his cap...'" (Levine)

Conversely, if an audience liked an actor, they would stop the show and make him sing a popular song. If the audience liked the actor playing Romeo, they would insist that he take the poison twice. The actor playing Romeo would be insulted if he wasn't asked to die by poisoning several times.

In addition to being unruly, early American theatre was also sophisticated. Shakespeare was the main attraction. In fact, Shakespeare was at the center of early American culture. Every cabin had the complete works of Shakespeare on its shelf. This was true in mining camps, on farms, and in Boston parlors. Everyone knew Shakespeare by heart, educated and uneducated alike.

A typical night at the theatre would look something like this: The evening would begin with an American farce, followed by the first two acts of *Richard III*. Then, the jugglers would come on stage, followed by Chinese dog tricks. Then, the rest of *Richard III* would be performed, ending with strong men doing physical stunts.

This format for theatrical performances was in place for over a hundred years until a class system began to emerge in the 1920's when Shakespeare was removed to expensive theatres for the educated class. "Legitimate theatre," or "art theatre," sought to present plays in their purity, without the jugglers and animal acts.

The idea behind the Art Theatre movement was that popular forms of entertainment were dangerous because they had the potential to infect and destroy higher forms of art. People looked upon Shakespeare as sacred and pure and the theatre as serious and lofty. Entertainment became a dirty word. A cultural hierarchy developed which continues to this day. The rich had their own theatres. Common folk were excluded through dress codes, ticket prices, and strict rules of behavior.

Several things struck me as I was exploring this early American material. The first is that when the theatre turns its back on the popular audience it loses its power to impact a culture. The reason that Jonathan had the impact he did was that theatre was at the center of early American society. It wasn't reserved for the educated and sophisticated classes. It was attended by everyone. I'm hard pressed to think of a single playwright today who has that kind of impact. By participating in and advocating an "art theatre" we have relegated ourselves to the margins. The result is that we don't impact the culture significantly. In the words of Ronald Davis, theatre has become "a symbol of culture, not a real cultural force" like it used to be in early America.

I also realized that the ability of the theatre to impact a culture is directly tied to the amount of pleasure and entertainment it provides. The day that theatre stopped providing the audience with a good time was the day we lost our power.

It was also the day the audience lost their willingness to embrace serious works. Don't forget that the centerpiece of those early American theatre performances were plays like *Richard III* and *Hamlet*. Walter Kerr writes about this in his book *The Theatre In Spite of Itself*: "The movement of theatre toward greater and greater seriousness and toward the responsibility demanded of it as a high art form has cut it adrift. We have paralyzed the theatre by our insistence that it take itself too seriously."

It also occurred to me that perhaps one of the reasons television is at the center of American culture today is that television programming has replicated the format of early American theatre performances. A perusal of prime time programs in the *TV Guide* reveals the same diversity of programming: there are sitcoms (farces), serious dramas and variety shows. There are animal acts, too: Stupid Pet Tricks on *David Letterman* and Wild Animals on *Jay Leno*. Obviously, this is a format that works.

Our early American playwrights understood this. So did the ancient Greeks. The Greek tragedies were performed with Satyr plays. And the Noh dramas of Japan always included a *kyogen* (comic) interval. Modern playwrights have foolishly forsaken this format in the name of art. If we want to recapture our audience, we should consider reviving it in some way.

My studies in early American theatre led me to think about the essence of popular culture and its role in the making of art. One of the main features of popular culture is that it throws things together with no apparent order and without regard to notions of purity, seriousness or excellence. I'm referring to the jugglers and *Richard III* sharing the same bill in early American theatre. Popular culture is a hodge-podge; it doesn't discriminate.

This hodge-podge is what the High Brow movement of the 1920's tried to eliminate. But something important happens when you put dancing dogs and farces on the same stage as *Hamlet*. They rub shoulders. Or hind ends. A conversation takes place. Not an *infection* that destroys the theatre, but a *pollination*, or a cross fertilization that keeps it alive, makes it stronger and helps it grow. As Walter Kerr remarks, "The seeds of great work come all too often from the slums."

Molière came out of folk farce. Kerr points out Leonard Bernstein maintained that opera developed out of *singspiel*—which is akin to musical comedy; and *Hamlet* owes his roots to Elizabethan horror fiction. The Noh drama of Japan began as "monkey music" in the fields. Many of Steven Sondheim's innovations came from "slumming" in the lower art forms—namely melodrama and the musical revue. And don't forget that it was Bert Lahr—who came from vaudeville—who was the best interpreter of Beckett's *Waiting for Godot*. As James Herne, a popular playwright from the 1920's observed, "when 'art' writers embrace popular 'lower' forms, innovation occurs and we end up getting popular drama plus."

I'm back in front of the classroom now, once again in the role of teacher. I am encouraging my playwriting students to use 19th century American theatre performance as a guide, to put jugglers in conversations with Shakespeare, and to let go of their aesthetic judgments. The high brow/low brow distinction has not served our theatre well. It's relegated us to the margins and impoverished our own work. I am urging them to change this.

I'm also encouraging them to make their work as big and broad as possible. Jonathan spoke to every region of the country and to every sector of society, and it's time that we do too. If playwrights want to be a cultural force, we must pay attention to what Kerr describes as the "natural appetite of the audience for a wide, constantly changing, unpredictable menu." And don't eliminate the sweets, he warns. Eclecticism and a hodge-podge of high and low forms is not a menace to the theatre's well-being or purity; rather, it is a sign of simple joy in the medium.

That joy keeps the theatre alive—and gives it the ability to leap, like Jonathan, off the stage and into the culture.

—*Delivered Summer, 2006, Plainfield, Vermont*

A BRIEF HISTORY OF ANYMORE

By Neil Landau

I.
I don't smoke pot.
Every day.
Anymore.

The only thing worse than having someone tell you "I don't love you"…
is having someone tell you "I don't love you anymore."

I've had both said to me.
And unsaid.

He took it back.
People can do that.
And what are we left with?
Except the scar tissue.
Your heart handed back to you in its original packaging.
More tender than it was.
Stronger than it will ever be.

We age.
The arteries harden, but if we're lucky, we become more vulnerable.

Pain begets compassion.
Even if everything hurts more.
We've learned how to muddle through.
Wisdom as panacea.

Grief is a memory buried in a minefield.
You never know when it's gonna blow.
Splatter. Ricochet. Shrapnel.
You can take it. You'll live.
Now there's just collateral damage
Where nothing matters

At least not on the outside
Anymore.

But then—it's inevitable—we open up again
To gather more data.
This can't be it.
There has to be something more.
There is.
But maybe only for someone else.
Maybe not for you
Anymore.

I stay tuned...
Even though I can't sit still or even listen so well anymore.

Too much static.
The war.
The pod person in the White House.
The hokey pokey on Capitol Hill.

Interest rates going up.
Polar ice caps melting down.
Issues, data, positions.

"They" tell us—the experts—to "live in the now."
But I'm never quite sure when now is.
Once I thought I knew, but then it whizzed on by.

If knowledge is wisdom and experience ripens us,
You'd think I'd have something to report.
But trust me: I'm unreliable.

When it comes to POV, we're all skewed.

II.

My current vantage point is midlife.
Okay, I'll come clean: midlife crisis.

My friend Allison is 47 and recently described a perky young actress
like this:
"She's in her 20s, you know, nothing really bad has happened to her yet."
I got what she meant—but in the context of Allison, whose
70-year-old mother's dying words to her were: "Don't put wet on wood."
Let's face it: the legacy of a once soggy now indelible glass ring on
furniture will outlive us all.
Only Allison doesn't get to endure her mother's words
Anymore.

Anymore implies once was.
You had something and lost it.
But sometimes that's positive:

I don't smoke cigarettes anymore.
I don't bite my nails anymore.
I don't give blow jobs to strangers in train stations anymore
(hypothetically).

For the artist: what's better: Has been or never was?
Reinvention can be integral to anymore.
Look at Madonna. Look at Cher. Look at Michael Jackson (bad example).

Still... they're all trying to endure. Just like us.

"I don't get upset about rejection anymore. Or critics. Or what anybody
says about me anymore"... implies evolution, self-assuredness,
maturity.
Or maybe you're just shut down. Maybe it's just stunted growth.
Which type of skin is better for an artist: thick or thin?
Thick implies a fortified castle.
Thin implies a glass house on a craggy hillside.

Which has greater visibility?
Which has more longitude?
Are we writing for us or for them?
I don't know anymore.

Maturity is all about anymore
As regrets pile up: things on Life's To-Do List That Still Aren't Done:
Golf lessons, piano, guitar, fluency in seven languages, scaling Everest.
Mid-life makes you come to grips with anymore.
Yearnings and procrastination become more, well, dire,
Along with the process of self-acceptance
And proficiency (or lack thereof) at letting go.

"My father is not alive anymore"... if said by a sixty-plus-year-old is more
or less expected, the natural order of things.
But if said by a six-year-old: a tragedy.

I've read that "tragedy plus time equals comedy."
But I don't get it.
Isn't "tragedy + time" just a tragedy that stings less?
Tragedy that isn't quite so horrific
Anymore?

Sometimes anymore is a rebellion, a visceral response to the
unimaginable.
To the Holocaust the signs proclaimed two immutable words:
Never Again.

III.

The memory is designed to decline as the body does.
Anger is an investment that festers, like the eye of a hurricane, then abates—breaks up—somewhere out in the sea of regret.

But leaves open the possibility of a held grudge:
"I'm not mad at you anymore because you're a fucking asshole."

Or morphs into apathy:
"I forgive you, but I don't care about you anymore."

"I have buried the hatchet because you're not worth axe-wielding for Anymore."

Peace and forgiveness intersect with anymore.

Besides, we're busier now.
Instant communication, instant gratification, instant replay on TiVo.
I've planted my flag in cyberspace.
I shop online. Bank online. Date online.
I don't ever have to leave the house anymore
If I don't want to.

It's hard to make a lasting human connection anyway
Anymore.
People already have their people.
Or have their people call my people.
At a certain age, some folks' lives are all filled up.
 "I barely have time to spend with my close circle anymore."

Everything's moving faster now. The celestial speedup.
But is life getting better or is it getting worse?

When I was in my twenties, I used to ask myself:
"How will I know when I've maximized my potential?
Will I get a sign, like a heart attack?"

Like my father did.
I was just six.
He was 39.

It left a void.
It just did.
It still hurts.

But now *I'm* a dad.
I tell my kids I love them.
They tell me back.

I wonder how they'll turn out.
And how long I'll get to stick around for the results.
And what will remain of me in them.

When I was 13, I used to wonder, in my darkest moments, how my life
might have turned out had my father lived.

I thought, maybe the road not taken was actually all happening in
some parallel universe,
And was convinced that other world would somehow be much better
than this one.

I don't anymore.

Only time will tell.
A legacy unraveled, sifted through.
Tears evaporate. Karma burns. Grudges thaw.

And what are we left with?
A shovel of dirt, a handful of ashes
Spirited away by an arid Santa Ana breeze.
Into the infinite expanse
Of anymore.

—*Delivered Summer, 2006, Port Townsend, Washington*

DR. EDIE GIVES A COMMENCEMENT SPEECH
By Paul Selig

(Dr. Edie, a happily disheveled woman in her fifties takes her place at a
podium festooned with flowers. She wears a ratty fur coat and a corsage.
She looks out at her audience with what can only be described as love.)

DR. EDIE

I have been told that today is a special occasion, so I have worn my rat.

All occasions are special to Dr. Edie Kelvin, but I am especially
honored because I have been told that I am here to address a room full
of people who hear voices.

I have not felt moved to don the skins of a dead animal since the
last time I took on a room, which was last Thursday, when I was escorted
bodily from a meeting of the American Psychiatric Association, of which
I am not a member, on the use of prescription drugs in medicating those
suffering from auditory hallucinations.

There, I was heard to scream loudly, "JOAN OF ARK WOULDA
BEEN ON PROZAK, MILTON WOULDA BEEN ON THORAZINE, AND
YOU COCKSUCKERS WOULD HAVE TAKEN THE CANDLES AWAY
FROM EDNA ST. VINCENT SO'S SHE COULDN'T BURN AT ALL."

I myself was born hearing voices. And I consider it to be quite a
privilege to be invited to share my story with you, who not only hear
them, but have the courage to follow what they say.

One winter, many years ago, when Dr. Edie was but a mite, her
voices guided her to the bus stop outside the Yeshiva to lie in wait for her
current beau, Morty Shine, the sexiest nine year old in Bensonhurst.

When Morty arrived, as the voices promised he would, little Edie
was horrified. For Morty appeared before her for the very first time
wearing glasses. Thick, ugly, bottle-busters with horned rims that lifted
the pais from the sides of his head so's he looked like the Hassidic Pippi
Longstockings.

Edie surveyed her ruined boyfriend, and a strange question
began to form in her mind. "Morty!" she said. "How did you know you
NEEDED them?"

And Morty reported the following:

He hadn't known he needed them. It wasn't until the Festival of Lights, when he had reached to ignite the candles and instead sent his sister up in flames, that his parents wondered if there might not actually be something physically wrong. Because little Shula Shine, though spindly in frame, did not in the least bit resemble their menorah.

Morty Shine, it was revealed, was nearly blind. He had been his whole life. He had actually managed to survive for nine years on a planet firmly believing that there were nothing but shadows beyond him. And what shocked Edie even more, was that up until that day, he had honestly thought that everyone else in the world saw that way too.

To say that this bit of information confused little Edie would be an understatement. For she had never before conceived of the notion of a "subjective" reality. She had assumed, like Morty, that everyone else thought exactly as she did. And she began to mistrust herself, worrying that perhaps she too was wrong, that she was deceived by what she saw... and heard...around her.

And as if enraged by her refusal to bear witness to her truth, the voices, which had always accompanied her through her days, began to turn...

And became cruel.

As Dr. Edie aged, they got louder. Harsh and horrible. They spoke of Dr. Edie's mistakes. Her failed marriage. Her unfinished dissertation. The child miscarried one night after an evening of ballroom dancing with a husband who was no longer hers. The voices told her that she was not enough, and Dr. Edie, frightened and alone, agreed.

In those days, Gawd spoke to her in different ways than he does now. He spoke to her in instances, unable to be heard through the clamor and din inside Dr. Edie's unprescribed head.

And the instances began to lead her, slowly, as she pulled herself through the thickness of days and the darkness of nights to a hotel room on West 72nd Street. Where the transients lived. Other women without settlements. Those whose voices had been silenced, by themselves and by a world that no longer believes that simply being a human being is cause enough for respect.

For some people are born with less skin than others. Some people are born with almost none at all. They bleed through their clothing as they walk down the street, and their eyes shine brightly in the anticipation of being struck.

Gawd spoke to Dr. Edie in instances then. Through signs. Through symbols. Through the changing of a streetlight that might lead her down an alley that might lead her to a stranger who might smile, in passing, with a kindness in the eyes...

And then one day, when she was lookin' to get in outa the rain, she found herself standing in the doorway of Teachers College. And Gawd spoke to her directly, saying "Enter, Edie Kelvin, for I have made you for this love..."

"You made me for what?" I said. "Gawd, you made me for this love?" And I said to him, "What is in it for me? Because being a cheerleader ain't my idea of success, and being kind ain't my idea of strength, and teaching the young five days a week ain't my idea of a high time, so's ya know."

Well, Gawd come back to me an' he said, "Edie, you have been created for this because you got the passion to prove me right. This is your own personal second coming. You got the knowledge of the night scares to make it better for them in the day, and they will recognize it. They will know it in your smile and see it in your eyes, that the pain of being can be mellowed into compassion."

And I screamed, "Gawd, you got the wrong chickie here. You got the wrong bird." And he said, "Who are you to tell me such things? You will do fine."

And so he sent me to Herbert Lehman High School in the Bronx, where the chairs in the faculty lounge ain't been upholstered since the WPA and the water fountain sends up blisters for fluid.

He sent me to Herbert Lehman High School, where the students are black, and much to Dr. Edie's horror all looked alike.

At first.

And then one day from her chalkboard she looked out across the sea of hope, and she began to notice how many shades of brown there were before her, and how much light was in the eyes of those she addressed, and how their potential radiated from them, like a flame threatening to devour her.

And she was humbled by this. She was humbled by their potential, and she was deeply ashamed at what she had done with her own. She had cried herself to sleep too many nights with what might have been, and there she was, now, confronted with the possibilities of what could be, might be, with a little bit of encouragement.

And she began to teach to their potential as if it was the most holy thing ever created. Because in Dr. Edie's mind it was holy. And she saw in each of them the tree that might grow from the seed, and she never once let that vision slip from her mind. And every day, her innocence was reborn. Every day she saw the potential in them, the beauty that was created in them come forth, she was reminded of her own.

And suddenly, the flame that had lain dormant and hidden inside her own bosom began to burn, and the voices that had always been there, censoring her, demanding her silence, one by one, began to sing...

"WEND YOUR WAY, BABIES," I say now, and I watch them stumble forward into their lives, and they are so very brave. They have such expectation on their faces. They have such hope in their hearts.

And I SEE myself standing onna mountain screaming out "WEND YOUR WAY BABIES," and I wave, and I clap, and I applaud for 'em all, because they are righteous in their being and they are noble in their efforts and they are loved, LOVED by Dr. Edie Kelvin. Because they are making their way back into the forest and she knows what lays ahead. And still they go. Still they go because they are young, and because they must. And if they choose to, they have each other, and that is a fine and righteous thing.

SO WEND YOUR WAY, BABIES. WEND YOUR WAY. And you're gonna cry sometimes, but that's part of it. Because this is a Big School and you grade yourself, so you might as well be generous in your assessment.

And if Dr. Edie could, she would walk before you. And she would bat away the terrors with the umbrella she carries with her always. She would beat away the monsters on the trail and she would make sweet beds of moss and leaves for her babies to lie in when they are tired.

But then she would not be a good teacher. Then she would not be wise and honor all the wisdom that she sees in her young.

So she prays at night for them. Loudly. And she celebrates them. Each and every mistake that is made along the way she applauds as loudly as the victories, because Dr. Edie KNOWS how learning occurs. And she says, "Lord, make their paths WIDE. No narrow paths for MY young. Make their paths WIDE and let them know all there is to know. And let them suffer and rejoice and grow wild in their own ways. But let them stay gentle. For gentleness is not weakness. It's an act of cowardice to be cruel, because you never gotta see the repercussions. People tend to cry in private, and by then you have turned away...

And those nights, when they come home from the jobs they said they'd never take, and they lay on their beds and think they are not enough, Dr. Edie will travel to them, travel through time and space with her rat flying and her umbrella beatin' at the wind, and say, "Oh, yes you are. Oh, yes you are."

And you write your poems on cocktail napkins. And you finish your novel in the attic room when the kids have gone to bed and the husband's had his fill. And you paint your pictures in grease on the skillet of the fast food if you have to, but then invite all the customers in to see.

And you tell your stories on the street corner, and at the tables in your twelve-step meetings, and to the cop who gives you the ticket, and to the doctor who threatens to put you away. But you are never silent.

And you pray at night for the courage to continue expressing your truth, and know that Gawd always answers a prayer like that. And know that your truth may change, as Dr. Edie's did, before she remembered who she was. Because Dr. Edie divorced herself many years ago, and has paid alimony for it ever since. But she is NOT PAYING ANYMORE, and she will NOT BE SILENCED.

And she will continue shouting her truth, until the men in white come and carry her off screaming and hollering, and she will wear her rat proudly from this day forth. For hers is a Holy War and she will always honor the voices that tell her where to turn...

And if you would accuse Dr. Edie Kelvin of being an idealist, just think for a moment, and know that you are the kind of person who believes that having an ideal is something to be accused of.

Because in the final analysis, babies, it's your own voices you gotta follow. Not old Dr. Edie's. She hears her own...

Let yours be kind ones.

—Delivered Winter, 1995, Plainfield, Vermont

VII. WRITING AND COMMUNITY

WHY I READ

by Elena Georgiou

At twenty-eight, in my second semester as an undergraduate in New York, in a class called The Nineteenth Century Novel, the professor began by asking us to write down our response to the following question: Why do you read? My answer was: To find community. This was a question to which I'd never before given any conscious thought; mine was a gut response I wouldn't have predicted. I knew the path I'd taken to arrive at this answer, however, and I knew how to retrace this path to find its origins.

As a young adult—from about fourteen to nineteen—I read and I read and I read. I came out of school with my 'A' levels, which, in England, means I opted to stay on for an extra two years to take the exams that would get me into university. By eighteen, I'd studied a handful of plays by Shakespeare, a couple of Thomas Hardy and Charles Dickens novels, Yeats' collected works, and a good number of other canonized texts. I loved them—they transported me to new and different worlds.

When I left school and opted to train as a dancer instead of pursuing English Literature at university, I kept reading. My reading list, though my own, was still heavily influenced by my education. I plowed my way through everything Thomas Hardy had written, and everything Emile Zola, Oscar Wilde, and D.H. Lawrence had written. My last memory of reading was lying on a beach in Cyprus, lapping up Dostoyevsky's *Crime and Punishment*. But soon after that, I stopped reading. At twenty, my love affair with books seemed to be over. This was not a conscious decision; the desire to read simply faded out of my life. I did not pick up a book again for five years. I remember, because when I did pick one up again, my life changed. I was twenty-five and lost, and someone who might have seen in me what I was missing gave me three books to read, books by people I'd never heard of, books by three American writers—Alice Walker, Toni Morrison, and Audre Lorde. I read until I fell asleep, and when I woke up I continued reading until I fell asleep again. In two days, I read these books and wept throughout the entire process. This was the first time I'd read about the lives of characters that in a significant way reflected my own experience. I had no idea that writing like this existed. Until reading these writers, I thought that everything I'd been feeling and thinking about the world was specific only to me. But here were the experiences of not one, but three writers who were creating characters and documenting lives with which I could identify. And they were still alive. And still writing. I couldn't believe it. How was it that we had so much in common? Why did this matter to me?

I was raised in an immigrant community that made it clear that even though London was where I was born, Cyprus—a place I'd visited a couple of times—was my home. I found this message impossible to live with. How could London not be home when it was the place where I was born, went to school, and was given my first library card? Then, my community's message was reinforced by a number of outspoken politicians who began movements that called for "repatriation;" that is, sending immigrants back to where they came from. But that didn't make sense to me either— London was where I came from. And then the National Front began marching through the streets, and putting human excrement through non-English peoples' mailboxes, and setting fire to one or two non-English peoples' homes. All in the name of keeping "England for the English." Then there were the words that I had to contend with on the way home from school: *Fuck off, Paki. Why don't you go back to your own country?* The first time this one was hurled in my direction, I was seven, and the full-grown man hurling the insult was up a ladder painting a house. I stood there for a minute staring at him, trying to make sense of what he was saying. I was not a Pakistani. And this was my home. *Go on,* he said. *Fuck off. Get out of here.* This, however, was not the incident that made the biggest impression. That incident did not contain words: It was Easter morning and I was with my sister and my mother and my grandmother and we were going to church. As we walked by a small house a few yards from the church, there was an old lady standing in her window, with the lace curtain pulled to one side. She had shaped her fingers into the back-to-front peace sign that in England means, "Fuck off." She kept waving her hand up and down in this menacing V, her face full of hatred. It was so incongruous—the lace curtain, the quaint house, the old lady, the contempt on her face, and the reversed peace sign telling me, once again, to: Fuck off back to my own country.

"Back to my own country." This was the phrase that linked me to the experiences that Lorde, Morrison, and Walker were documenting. These three writers were writing about people who were living in their own countries, when their own countries did not want them—they were writing about colonized people, dispossessed people, people who were not valued by the dominant society that told them that no matter what they looked like or how they acted, they would never belong. Reading about this unbelonging helped me to try to make sense of my own unbelonging. For the first time in my life, in the characters in novels, in poems, and in essays, I felt as if I saw versions of myself. It changed my relationship to reading; whereas previously I was reading to escape into different worlds, now I was reading to learn about my own world via characters that made me feel as if I had a right to exist. This was partly what I meant when I answered the way that I did to the question: Why do you read. But there was more to my answer. Reading these three books also prompted me into an awakening— it introduced me to the idea of what it meant to be a colonized person.

Being a colonized person within an immigrant community is a lose-lose situation. You are damned if you are invisible and you are damned if you are visible. Because I did not look like the proverbial English Rose, I was invisible to much that could have had a positive impact on my life. And again, because I did not look like the proverbial English Rose, I was a target to much that was negative. It was a relatively schizophrenic existence: how would I be perceived today? Invisible or visible?

The process of my decolonization began with an attempt to deconstruct the person that I was told I was and continued in a search for how I wanted to be perceived. Instead of others—family, community, politicians, random hostile strangers—supplying me with a ready-made label, I wanted to create my own personhood, one that made sense to my experience of the world.

I was born in 1961, the year after Cyprus gained its independence from Britain. But even though the place of my ancestors was no longer colonized, and even though I spent no more than two weeks on the island every few years, I had inherited the legacy of a country that had been colonized a couple of times by the Greeks, a couple of times by the Turks, and a couple of times by the British. (In fact, if you trace the country's history, it has been colonized eleven times, and has only known fourteen years of complete independence). The Greek dialect that Greek-Cypriot people speak is considered to be the lowest form of the language. If you couple this information with the fact that all mother-tongues stagnate whenever a group of people immigrate to another country, you should imagine me standing on the lowest rung of a linguistic ladder. And then, just when I thought I couldn't get any lower, my English was not the Queen's English; it was the English of Pearly royalty—my accent belonged to the House of Cockney, *not* the House of Windsor. In England, identifying class by accents is learned at birth; therefore, I knew from an early age that all my ways of speaking were stigmatized. But in 1987, after the work of Lorde, Walker, and Morrison had opened my mind, I began to read writers who were challenging the ideas of class and race that up until that time had formed my way of thinking. The following year, I left England and enrolled at the Hunter College of City University of New York. (An institution, that unbeknownst to me at the time of enrollment, had Audre Lorde as a professor in the English department).

As an undergraduate, one of the first books I studied at college was Ngugi Wa Thiongo's *Decolonizing the Mind*. Once again, here was another writer from another country, and another continent, talking about experiences that were almost identical to my own. Next came books like *The Wretched of the Earth* by Frantz Fanon, *Pedagogy of the Oppressed* by Paolo Freire, *This Bridge Called My Back* by Gloria Anzaldua and Cherrie Moraga, *A Small Place* by Jamaica Kincaid, and *Woman, Native, Other* by Trinh T. Minh-ha. I kept reading, I kept studying, I kept working at decolonizing my mind. Eventually, I graduated with a degree that focused heavily on the post-colonial experience. I also graduated with a community of friends who had read similar books and wrestled with similar ideas. Once again, through reading, I'd found community.

Today, almost twenty years later, this is no longer the only reason I read. At this stage in my life, I've found not only community, but also communities. Plus, I am actively engaged in and even earning a living from a passion that directly relates to reading—writing. And so, if you asked me right now why I read, I would probably answer: To be inspired.

As a writer, I think of my body as a well that is mostly filled through reading. I read books to collect images. I read books to collect specifics. I vary what I read to make sure that my well is not filled with one type of text; for example, I choose to read about science, about anthropology, and about art forms other than writing. For the past ten years, to keep my life as a teacher and as a writer in balance, there are certain times of the year when I sequester myself to write. I go away from home and I make sure my bag is packed with a selection of varied reading material. I take novels, poetry books, sometimes a memoir, and always some books that fall under the enormous category of non-fiction. And because I am writing away from home, most often this means I also have access to a selection of books that I would not have chosen for myself. I love this exposure, this randomness, the surprise of being engaged in unplanned reading. As I write this essay, I am staying in a house owned by a couple of visual artists and some of the books I have access to are *The Art and Craft of Stonework, Dogs Behaving Badly, The Mushroom Trailguide, The Shape of Time*, and *The Artist as Outsider*. Some of the books I brought with me are *Walden, The Body, Uses of the Brain,* and *Life is Elsewhere*. I'm hoping that by the time I've read through these books I will not only have digested some of what they have to tell me, but I will also have stolen a few of their images, some of their phrases, and perhaps even learned a new word or two. I'm also hoping that by the end of this trip I will come away with at least one or two moments of inspiration to keep me writing.

At this point in my life, reading is less about escape, less about finding community, and mostly about what is being said, how it is being said, and what new information I can garner and use. Reading has become a place of work, a place to study craft, to think about voice, to search for my own vision. But fortunately, there are also many moments when reading is still a way to leave the world I am familiar with and enter into another world that is inspiring and new.

—*Delivered Winter, 2006, Plainfield, Vermont*

EVERYTHING IS FREE NOW

By John McManus

When I was seventeen and a freshman in college, my first writing teacher, Madison Smartt Bell, asked each person in our fiction workshop to make a list of his or her ten favorite books. After we'd done so, he collected them. Without commenting on the lists or even looking at them he sealed them in an envelope, thanked us, put it in his briefcase, and moved on. When someone asked, "Why'd you do that?" Madison looked around, let out one of his deep, sinister chuckles, and said, "It's an experiment I like to conduct."

Before long I determined that its purpose had been to make us feel, if not self-conscious about our choices, at least defensive about whether they were good ones. Mine weren't, I decided after having spent a few weeks around other freshmen who, like me, wanted to be writers. I'd just arrived at college from the kind of rural high school where the coach who taught world history told us that there were two kinds of Muslims: the Sunnies and the Shitties. I sauntered onto my college campus figuring I knew more than other people; instead I learned that Proust wasn't pronounced Prowst and that you weren't supposed to think *The Prince of Tides* was a good book. Eventually I went to Madison and asked for my list back.

"Why?" he asked.

"I made a mistake," I said. But he wouldn't give it to me.

Some of us who want to publish writing might be loathe to admit that we want to in part for selfish reasons: we want to transmit more memes than we've been transmitting. We want to steal the reins of the zeitgeist away from Insert Name of Hated But Celebrated Young Wunderkind and put them in the hands of people who bleed when pricked and who have worked for a living. We want, when we read in the latest *New Yorker* that "she said, sighing, and walked across the room," to neutralize the poison of that phrase by reaching for a text whose antivenin will derive its strength from the absence of such banalities, but that text has become hard to find on the new bookshelf at Barnes & Noble or Borders—which want to combine, by the way, so that they can control the dissemination of information in this country—because publishers value marketability, which in literary fiction these days seems to my perhaps envious eyes to mean cleverness, preciousness, adherence to trends.

Some of those "Brooklyn Books of Wonder," as they were called in my favorite essay of 2007, are about more than irony, but they're rarely about what it means to be human, to feel oneself borne up by jealousy and hate and love and grief. I imagine their fans would mock my sincerity in saying so. But who am I to say? Last year I went to France to rewrite a novel of mine at a place called Camargo, where, along with twelve other very lucky people, I was given an apartment with sweeping views of the sea and a sheer limestone face called Cap Canaille that rose up out of it. Every morning the sun would rise over Cap Canaille while I sat scribbling away at a book that I hoped would change how Americans conceived of this, that, and the other. It would be an indictment of the war. It took as its conceit that a terrorist organization called the Order of the Ibex has for centuries used its understanding of quantum physics and many-worlds theory to shape history by means of writers and artists whom it kidnaps and forces to dream up particular scenarios, thus causing the fictional events they've described to come true in other quantum universes. It would probe the failure of contemporary artists to effect political change in America. I wrote that in a grant application: *probe the failure of contemporary artists to effect political change in America.* I wrote it in another application and another and even mentioned it in my bio on Goddard's website. Some part of my mind was aware that a book with seven point-of-view characters, none of whom is quite a goal-oriented protagonist and five of whom are gay, would not under *normal* circumstances be considered commercial enough to *make a dent in the American consciousness*, yet I would look out at the sunsets reflected in ochre on the limestone above water the color of blue Kool-Aid and know that everything would work out. I reminded myself to hurry, so that the thing could be published before the 2008 election.

George Garrett wrote an essay about an editor who warned him that a book of his lacked the forward propulsion necessary to "make a dent in the American consciousness." They would go around and around, he and the editor, and every few days the editor would come back to that phrase: *dent in the American consciousness*. Garrett said that he eventually came to think of the American consciousness as a huge old green '56 Chevrolet, with a gigantic, gleaming, immaculately undented bumper taunting him in front.

In 2004, Nicholson Baker set out to make a dent in the American consciousness. He published a book called *Checkpoint*, in which two men sit around a Washington, D.C., hotel room—a room in the Watergate, no less—and plot how to kill the president. Not just any president. They sit talking about how to kill George W. Bush. They contemplate killing other administration figures as well, and name them by name. The plot is fairly conventionally straightforward, but the execution is as inventive as they come. I was living in Berlin when it came out, and I read the whole thing while sitting in a bookstore. By the end I was downright giddy thinking about the debate that was going to arise out of it. I knew it was illegal to even suggest killing the president. 'Nicholson Baker has probably been arrested,' I thought. 'He's probably in jail, and maybe other writers are trying to get him out, and there will be some groundswell of support that will snowball into an actual protest movement that prominent American writers will *actually get involved in*, the way Norman Mailer and Robert Lowell did in *The Armies of the Night*.' But there weren't any protests. Nicholson Baker wasn't arrested. Why? Because what Nicholson Baker had done was write a work of literary fiction, and for reasons that I unfortunately think include its being that—a work of literary fiction—it did not make a dent in the national consciousness.

I don't set out to write hard books. I don't want my prose to be difficult or labyrinthine or baroque or anything but clear and lucid. If I were good at writing simple, straightforward stories, I'd do it—and I bet if I were good at it I'd enjoy doing it, too, because I'd be good at it. But as it stands, what I enjoy doing is creating intricate logic puzzles and then trying to solve them, holding ideas up to the light and scraping away at them at an oblique angle, rather than charging forward headlong into them. At some level, beneath the heady optimism, I knew while I sat at that desk in the South of France that I was writing a book most people would consider hopelessly uncommercial. I could tell because some of the influences on its conception were the journeys in place and thought of W.B. Sebald in *The Rings of Saturn*; the musings by the fictional writer Elizabeth Costello in J.M. Coetzee's book by that name on whether the canon, by imitating itself so often, engages in a sort of duplicative fading; and the aggressive alienation of Bruno in Michel Houellebecq's *The Elementary Particles*.

Those three novels are ones I love because they take fundamental risks at their very premise that allow them to tell stories in new ways. Almost all my favorite books are ones that find new ways to tell stories. When I started getting serious about writing, I had a lot of stubborn, self-righteous notions, and one was that if you're not changing the nature of storytelling, you're not doing anything worthwhile. I would hold up a conventionally told story and say, "Why should anyone remember this in 500 years?" I pooh-poohed the notion that any number of great American writers like John Updike, Philip Roth, or Saul Bellow were any good. I loved Cormac McCarthy, and then when he started getting popular I had some knee-jerk notion that he was "selling out": once everyone knew who he was, I didn't want to call him my favorite anymore. He'd finally sunk his mallet into the chrome bumper of that old green Chevrolet, which somehow made him conventional so that I stopped trusting him and turned for comfort to more obscure writers who couldn't afford their rent and ate their meals off the free-sample trays at grocery stores. But McCarthy didn't stop being good. When he appeared on *Oprah* last year, his televised visage didn't beam itself back through time into the original text of *Blood Meridian* to make it less powerful or startling or strange. There were still those amazing favorite lines of mine:

> "And now the horses of the dead came pounding out of the smoke and the killing ground and clattered from sight again. Dust stanched the wet and naked heads of the scalped who with the

fringe of hair below their wounds and tonsured to the bone now lay like maimed and naked monks in the bloodslaked dust and everywhere the dying groaned and gibbered and horses lay screaming."

So I got back from France and sent my big inventive political novel to my agent, and he went on vacation and came back and went on another vacation and another until three months had gone by and I gave up on waiting and called him—and he wanted me to rewrite a certain part of it. That meant it wouldn't be making its dent in the American bumper before the '08 election, but he'd said enough nice things about it that I was placated, and anyway there were signs that whenever it came out, 2009 or 2029, there would still be a war raging.

But then around Halloween I happened to speak to him again. He'd been talking to my former editor at Picador—not on my behalf, but I guess I came up in conversation, and the editor mentioned he wished I would write something along the lines of *The Beach*. He'd already said so to me thirty-seven times: why not write *The Beach*? Wouldn't it be nice if you wrote *The Beach*? In case you're not familiar with this book, it's the novel by Alex Garland that was marketed as THE FIRST GREAT NOVEL ABOUT GENERATION X. It was made into a movie starring Leonardo DiCaprio as a young, hot, edgy backpacker who meets up with some other hot, edgy backpackers in Thailand. The three proceed to do some edgy visceral things like have sex and do drugs. If this is anyone's favorite novel, I offer my apologies for not liking it, but I've tried each time it was cited to me as a model for emulation. Each time I failed. So finally this time I threw my arms up and demanded, "You don't like this book, I don't like it, and my editor doesn't even like it, so why are we all holding it up as an example?" And my agent thought a minute and said, "Well, Alex Garland was a young guy when he wrote it, and you're a young guy, and it's a simple straightforward story about young people behaving badly in a world without boundaries."

I paused and said, "So you want me to write a simple straightforward story about young people behaving badly in a world without boundaries?" And he said, "Now you're just making fun of me." And I said, "No, I'm just trying to understand what you want me to do!" And he said, "Then yes, that's what I want you to do."

Now, the same part of me that used to throw at walls books I thought weren't ambitious enough to be remembered after a millennium wanted to throw the phone against the wall, too, and give up writing and go work at the Dairy Queen—but another part of me wanted to say, "Oh yeah? I can do that." It so happened I was running the New York Marathon the following day. Somewhere in Harlem between miles twenty-two and twenty-three in an utter delirium, or should I say moment of clarity, I came up with a way to combine some ideas that had been festering and then the day after that went to Yaddo where in another idyllic room that looked out on rows of hickories still shedding their few last leaves, I started a new book that I worked on furiously until there was a foot of snow and that I can't coherently describe to you except to say it's a simple, straightforward story about young people behaving badly in a world without boundaries.

But is it a simple straightforward conventional story?

I don't put an exclamation point after the word 'No!' because I'm opposed to conventions. Five hundred years—I mean, who did I think I was? If Nicholson Baker made no impact because only a select few read literary fiction and the dominant narrative art form is soon to switch to video-blogging, *none* of it will last, neither the best examples nor the worst, which frees us to do whatever we want. If people are likely to care about a particular book in the distant future, maybe it's too far ahead of its time to reach a wide audience in this market, which means it will never be born into the world as a document for readers in our future to potentially care about. Quite a paradox—yet I look around this room and see how dynamic and alive is literary America: we're over a hundred people, and we're one of hundreds of writing programs creating a community of writers and readers tens of thousands strong who do this because we love it and because we need to. And if each of us—the people in this room and our counterparts around the country—bought fifty books a year, then we, the students and graduates and faculty of American MFA programs, could single-handedly create enough demand to marshal into this world plenty of published work too high in quality for anyone in the far future to imagine it ever stood a chance of not existing.

And if another Great Depression hits and each of us buys zero books a year, and then E-books take over and everyone downloads them for free as bit torrents and burns copies of them like CDs—think how ominous that is: "I'll burn you a book"—we'll all forge on anyway because we love it and we need to.

—*Delivered Winter, 2008, Plainfield, Vermont*

CROSSING THE LINE:
LANGUAGE, LIVES, STORIES
By Juliana Spahr

As the months went by, they found themselves thinking hard about how to negotiate things, about analogy, about the word we, about how to be in a place that was so not for them. We was undeniably a contested word for them. They often felt huge in it, huge because there were three of them instead of two. But they also found that they could not *not* think of these things all the time because it was constantly pointed out to them by others that they were not from the island in the middle of the Pacific, and further, that they were there on the island only because of a history of imperialism and colonialism that favored them. For instance, shortly after they arrived one of them went to a rally at the university where one of them worked that was happening to protest the latest round of budget cuts. On the island in the middle of the Pacific, the budget cut protest, like most budget cut protests, turned quickly from a protest about budget cuts to a protest about other things. In this case, the protest became about the hiring practices of the university, which hired almost exclusively people from various continents and very few people from any islands, not only few from the one on which the university was located but also few from any other islands in the Pacific. At the protests, a student leader who had genealogical ties to the island from before the whaling ships arrived gave a speech against budget cuts and she concluded her speech by offering to buy any *haole* professor who wanted one a one-way ticket off the island. When they heard this speech at first they cringed. They cringed not because they were angry. It was instead a cringe of recognition. A cringe that the university did not hire fairly and that they themselves had gotten their job because of the unfair hiring practices of the university. They cringed because they agreed and because they agreed they longed to follow after her and ask for their ticket back to someplace. But then they wondered to what place? What would be the proper destination for the ticket? Did they belong on the continent, where they had been born? But they were in some sense new to the continent. They and their parents had been born on the continent, but none of their parents' parents had been born there and the continent too had a history of arrival by people from afar who came and acted as if the place was theirs.

This issue of where they should be on the bus, in the room, on the globe, this issue of belonging, felt often like it hit them in the gut, by which they meant it hit them where it mattered, it hit them in the palm of their writing hand, in that space that their little and ring fingers made when they held a pen, the space that when they were learning to write in first grade they had been forced to fill with a small cool marble so as to learn the proper way of holding a pen.

At times they felt as if they could chart out the options for writers who, like them, had arrived from afar. The chart would begin with two categories: writers from afar who dealt with the island in their writing and writers from afar who did not. Then each of these two categories could be further broken into two other categories. The writers from afar who did not deal with the island category would become split into writers from afar who did not deal with the island in their work because they thought the island and its culture were small and uninteresting, and writers from afar who did not deal with the island in their work because they felt that anything they might say as someone who came from afar would just further cultural appropriation. So in other words the neutral category of dealing with the island or not in their writing would become split into those who did this out of disregard and those who did this out of respect. Similarly, among those who were from afar and who dealt with the island in their writing, there would also be two other sub-categories: those from afar who felt they could just deal with the island because they were there, that when they moved to the island from afar they gained the right to talk about it, and those from afar who felt they had no right but the responsible thing to do in their writing was to talk about the island, especially to write about how the island was colonized in order to keep stating this thing because so many people on the continent over-looked this colonization. This last sub-category, the category first of writers from afar who wrote about the island and then the sub-category of those who felt that they had a responsibility to write about how the island was colonized in their writing and yet also that they had to constantly position themselves as not from the island, was often accompanied by an endless self-reflection in which those that held this position felt they had to constantly position themselves in their writing as from afar. They themselves were in this last category. But they did not think that their position on this chart was necessarily the correct position. If they knew anything at all, they knew they could never fully avoid the many problems of being a writer from afar in a place so colonized. But they also felt that they had to act as if it might be possible to write something that was not the wrong thing because to not act as if that might be possible was to risk being even more a part of the problem. They did not want to be like those who had a dismissive lack of interest in the island, or like those who were filled with anger at the island because the island induced in them funny feelings of being out of place and strange or made them think about things they would rather not think about such as how they were seen as colonizers in this place

On top of all this anxiety, they added more. They also knew that they were not only writers from afar, but they were writers who wrote in the language that had had a long colonial history, an expansionist language that was spreading to more and more places every day. The resonances of this expansion were especially felt in their time, a time in which more and more languages were disappearing every day, disappearing so quickly that some predicted that at least ninety percent of the languages in the world would disappear in the next hundred years. They themselves knew this expansionist language as their first language because of its expansionism. They had learned this language from birth and their parents had learned it from birth, but their grandparents had learned other languages at birth and came later to the expansionist language, except for one grandmother who had learned the expansionist language because the island on which she had been born had been coerced to give up its language in 1801 by a nation that spoke the expansionist language.

On the island in the middle of the Pacific, this expansionist language had arrived on the whaling ships. Many of the people who lived on the island, not only those from afar but also those born on the island but with parents or grandparents from afar and also those with genealogical ties to the island from before the whaling ships arrived, spoke this language. Many people told one another that they loved one another in this language. And many wrote their grocery lists in this language. And many called out to one another in this language when they saw one another on the street and got angry and screamed out their anger with each one in this language. And when they worked fifteen-hour days in the service industry, they worked them most often in this language. And even when they chatted with one another in a creole as they sat around talking, drinking beers, and eating plates of meat and rice on their lanais at night, the creole they spoke, while it was undeniably its own language, was very close to this expansionist language. They did this even though there had been a perfectly good language on the island for many years before the whaling ships arrived, a language that most human ears heard as unusually beautiful.

Some called this expansionist language a cultural bomb. And they could see all the ways this might be true on the island. The expansionist language was so good at circumference that it often absorbed in order to kill out the language that had been there before the whaling ships arrived. And it also slowly expanded over the languages that were often created by its arrival, the pidgins and creoles, the burrowing languages, the negotiating languages. For instance, the creole that many people born on the island spoke when talking to other people also born on the island was so close to this expansionist language because the expansionist language was slowly taking over the mix of different languages that had originally formed the creole. The expansionist language expanded regularly and steadily. This expansion was not innocent. The expansionist language had become the language that most people spoke not because it was more beautiful and not because it was easier and not because it had more literature but because of a law that from 1896–1970 had banned the language that had been spoken on the island for many years before the whaling ships arrived. But the expansionist language continued to expand so well not only because of these laws, but also because of the legacies of nineteenth century imperialism: the coercive economic dominance of the nations who spoke the expansionist language, the military might of the nations who spoke the expansionist language, and the technology industry and its alliances with the entertainment industry both of which conducted almost all of their business in the expansionist language and offered up tepid and narrative-based stories about modernity that most humans found somewhat pleasant.

And yet, despite the expansionist language and all its tools, all the laws and all the imperialism, all the economic dominance, all the military might, all the technologies, and all the entertainments, the language politics of the island remained endlessly complicated. The expansion did not happen overnight and one could point for many years to how the language that had been there before the whaling ships arrived and the languages that were often created by the arrival of the expansionist language to some place new, the pidgins and creoles, the burrowing languages, the negotiating languages refused to go away as evidence of how the expansionist language might not be as good at expansion as one might think. Undeniably, the expansion took some time, some generations. It was often contested. Often it would expand and manage almost to kill a language and then the language would rise up again and reassert itself. But despite the resurgence of the language that had been there before the whaling ships arrived on the island, the expansionist language continued to expand and at its best it brokered an uneasy peace with the language that had been there before the whaling ships arrived and allowed the language to exist beside it, claiming the business of the technology industry and the entertainment industry for itself and yet allowing some songs to be sung and some poems and stories to be written in either or both the language that had been there before the whaling ships arrived and the languages that were often created by the arrival of the expansionist language, the pidgins and creoles, the burrowing languages, the negotiated languages; on the island, it even allowed a few classrooms to be taught in the language that had been there before the whaling ships arrived.

They knew that the problem with the expansionist language was not just the cultural bomb problem. It was not just the expansionist language that was the problem. After all, culture happened even in the expansionist language. They themselves were fine with how the language they had learned from birth was the expansionist language even though they had no geological ties to the people who had felt that this language was their own. They had not wished that their lullabies were in another, truer language when they were children. They had never felt that they could not love their mothers or each other enough because the various names by which they called their mothers and each other were in the expansionist language. And if they looked at the histories of any location they saw poems and songs thriving and surviving any change of language. The culture might change, the poems and songs might rhyme differently or form different patterns to better meet the sounds of the language, but no matter what, any language was fully capable of expressing the special emotions that tended to come with having to negotiate an oppressive and foreign government on one's own land, an intense anger towards those from afar combined with a love of those near, plus a love of the land and a love of the things on the land, a love say of how the *kukui* clustered in vein-like streams down the crevice of a ravine. Nor was it that the language that was there before the whaling ships arrived and the languages that were often created by the arrival of the expansionist language to some place new, the pidgins and creoles, the burrowing languages, the negotiating languages were necessarily libratory. They heard too many homophobic and racist poems in those languages to think this was only about language.

But they understood still how this did not mean that they wanted someone to come from afar and make them train their children in a language from afar so that their children would whisper in their lovers' ears in a language that was the language of those from afar. It was as those optical illusions that had so mesmerized them as a child. If they looked one way, they saw the face, they saw reasons not to care. If they looked the other way, they saw the vase, they saw reasons to care.

Yet despite this back and forth, they felt that nothing was innocent, that when they wrote their poems, their essays, their software programs, their notes in the expansionist language, they immediately became not only a part of the expansionism by the accident of birth but they became willful agents of expansionism. When they wrote, they wrote as war machine. When they wrote, they wrote as ideological state apparatus. When they wrote, they wrote as military industrial complex. This list went on and on. They wrote as colonial educational system. They wrote as the bulldozing of the land and the building of unnecessary roads. They wrote as the filling in of wetlands with imported sand to build beaches. And they wrote as the ever expanding tourist industry. And while all of them were well schooled in the avant garde, an avant garde that used fragmentation, quotation, disruption, disjunction, agrammatical syntax, and so on to make them like a foreigner in their own language, they were finally not all that sure that using fragmentation, quotation, disruption, disjunction, agrammatical syntax, and so on escaped any of the expansionism. They wanted to believe the avant garde claim that they could write so as to move between the borders of languages, that they could write beyond the duality of metaphors if they kept piling them up, one on top of another, that they could write from third spaces, that they could write so as to abolish colonialism if they did not use narrative continuity. And yet they also felt that this was somewhat absurd.

At moments all this feeling, all this burrowing and negotiating made them feel optimistic and vaguely excited. It was like the sun in this place. The sun was bright and stimulating. It was an antioxidant and produced melanin in their skin that in turn blocked ultraviolet rays. It felt good to be out in the sun and they liked to feel the sun heating up their skin, feel its stimulation, feel it causing some sort of chemical reaction that relaxed their muscles, their brain, and then filled them with small feelings of mild euphoria. And their feeling that they might some day figure things out if they kept thinking about things with generosity and an open mind and heart was to them an antioxidant and a protectant and yet another small feeling of mild euphoria. But they also knew that because they were from afar and because their relatives were from afar they could not stay too long in the sun thinking and trying to figure things out no matter if they did it with generosity or if they did it with anger as the rays would injure their blood vessels and swelling and reddening would result.

After spending days which turned into months and then months which turned into years out in the sun of complication, a sun which exposed the very language they had learned from birth as not natural but as expansionist and a sun which complicated poetry, they developed not only the reddening of a sunburn but also the dry mouth and throbbing head of heat stroke. So they began to make up a series of rules hoping they would work as a tree that might somewhat shade them and would as a result allow them to stay out in the sun thinking. Their rules went like this... Whenever they discussed the island, they had the responsibility to address the legacy of colonialism in the island. They could never pretend that it did not shape their every sentence, their use of every word, their every comma, and their every period. They could not pretend that they were innocent of it, that they did not benefit from it all the time. They felt that any work that they did about the island should somehow make clear that it was against colonialism. But at the same time this work should also make clear that they were not the only person who had ever thought up anticolonialism. They had to both point out that they supported the sovereignty movement and that this movement was larger than them and that while they supported the movement they were not its spokesperson and were not a major or crucial part of this movement. And they felt that they should never suggest in their work that they knew what form of government the people who had genealogical ties to the island from before the whaling ships arrived should use but they also felt that they should suggest as often as possible that the island should be governed by those who had genealogical ties to the island from before the whaling ships arrived and not by those from afar. They also felt they should not claim to understand the culture that was there before the whaling ships arrived. And if they were for some reason going to write something set in the past, they should not set any of their work in the time before the whaling ships arrived. And they felt they should make clear in their work that they were in dialogue with other writers from the island, they were not the only writer from the island or even the writer to read when one wanted to read about the island and that this dialogue might not even be dialogue because it might just be that they were influenced, not that they actually influenced anyone back. They felt they had to make clear when talking to people that their perspective on the island was just one among many and an incomplete one that they arrived at only by learning from others who had genealogical ties to the island from before the whaling ships arrived and others who were born on the island but had families and heritages from afar. So they wrote no poems about how beautiful the bougainvillea was without also mentioning how the plant was probably brought to the island in 1827 by Father Bachelot, the first catholic missionary to the island. And during this time whenever they had to submit a biographical note to go with some publication they always wrote that they were a continental *haole* so as to make clear that they did not have genealogical ties to the island from before the whaling ships arrived, but the editors of the publications on the continent kept editing out this information.

They did not think that their rules should be everyone else's rules or that other people had to sign on to them. They did not nail them to any door. And they made it a point not to complain about other people's differing rules. They respected the decision of their friend not to teach creative writing, even though they felt that creative writing at the university could not change unless people who felt that it should be taught by those with genealogical ties to before the whaling ship arrived taught it and then worked to hire those people, because it would not do this hiring without internal pressure. It for sure was not going to change on its own. And they let their rules evolve and change over time. At some moments letting themselves mention the bougainvillea as if it was innocent or perhaps skirting into dangerous territory by using the names of the animals and plants mentioned in a creation chant that was composed before the whaling ships arrived in their own work. At other moments they found themselves suddenly inserting the words of plants or animals in the language that was spoken in the island before English. Words like *mai`a, `ulu, kukui,* and *ti* would suddenly appear in a poem about what people might carry with them. Or they found themselves describing themselves and people like them through metaphors of invasive alien plants. Like *koa haole* and *huehue haole*. And also trees like *kiawe*, which was brought to the island in the 1800s and grew so out of control that it was responsible for lowering the water tables all over the island. They justified this by saying that the ecological model of the chant fascinated them and that ecology was so crucial it transcended culture, no one could own that field of knowledge. But they also recognized how they had broken one of their rules.

Sometimes others saw the rules and their continued desire to discuss the rules as guilt. So they thought a lot about guilt during this time. They began by thinking what is wrong with guilt. After all, they were guilty of so many things. It was an endless list but right at the top of their list was the large amount of protein they and those in their nation ate, the large amount of oil they and those in their nation used, the large amount of pollutants they and those in their nation put in the air and in the ocean and on the land, the large number of people that had been killed in the name of freedom for them and those in their nation. They wondered if guilt was bad because it was an emotion of inaction, if it was really just all talk and no action as was often said. But they also thought that part of the reason things were so wrong was that not enough people felt guilty. And then they also noticed that the charge of guilt was used more often to stop people from action and conversely that guilt often moved people to action. And then they moved from thinking about guilt to thinking about complicity. Because what they really wanted was to constantly be saying they were complicit with all sorts of things, things that happened without their consent but happened nonetheless and continued to happen also without their consent. And they could not figure out how to make clear to everyone that these things were happening without their consent other than to just keep saying it over and over in their small and ineffective voices.

But at times, despite their attention to the rules, despite all their attempts to find firm footing for themselves around this issue of appropriation, they found themselves at moments feeling as if they could never find their way. One afternoon they went to an all-day conference at the university on globalization and at the conference a woman who had genealogical ties to the island from before the whaling ships arrived spoke and she said that she felt that the university should not allow anyone to write on the people or the culture of the people who had genealogical ties to the islands before whaling ships arrived. She called on the university to set up rules that said that any such work should have to be approved by a board made up of people who had genealogical ties to the island from before the whaling ships arrived. They wondered as they listened to her talk if her talk was more rhetorical than anything else. She was after all requesting that the university commit huge infringements on the first amendment rights of state workers and her request was impossible to enforce. But her saying this made them feel nervous about their own work despite all the time they had spent obsessively thinking and revising their rules. They could just dismiss her. Just say she was yet another example of ethnic nationalism and look what ethnic nationalism had done to the twentieth century. But they felt that this dismissal would also be missing a point, or a series of complicated points about the long history of constant yet profoundly unequal exchanges that had defined the thinking on and about the island. They felt that at this moment they could never have enough rules. They felt caught. They felt caught between their feeling that the responsible thing to do was to be attentive to the issues that so defined the island and yet they also worried that they had no right to talk about the island. They felt as if they could not escape, whatever they did was wrong. And this feeling of never enough rules overwhelmed them into a sort of depressed inaction and they realized that despite the rules they had spent obsessively thinking and revising they had trouble answering hard yet obvious questions about their work. When a friend asked them who they wrote for, they realized that they barely thought about this question and it was hard to figure out the answer. They finally admitted that they guessed they wrote for themselves. They wrote for themselves because they wrote to figure out things that they could not figure out otherwise, things they could not figure out just by thinking. They needed writing. They needed poetry because it reshaped their mind, because it re-sorted things in different, sometimes beautiful, sometimes troubling patterns. They needed poetry to think with others, to think with the traditions of the island, to think beside them and near them but not as part of them. They wished they could say that they wrote for themselves and for strangers. But it seemed presumptuous to say they wrote for strangers, at least for strangers on the island. They agreed with their friend that if they wrote about another culture, an at-risk culture because of colonialism and a culture that was not theirs really, the writing should give something back to the culture. But it also felt presumptuous to think they could give anything back. The culture was so rich and so complete without them.

At this same conference on globalization a man who, like them, was from afar but who had lived on the island for many years gave a talk. His talk was about the ocean. He had an understanding of the ocean as also at risk, but at risk because of human interference and human refusal to see the connections between all the parts of the ocean. He saw clearly how humans refused to understand that when they dumped waste into one part of the ocean they dumped it into all of the ocean; how when they fished out one part of the ocean, they fished out the entire ocean. He ended his talk by begging them to remember the ocean, to just remember the ocean amidst all their fighting. And at this time they found this so moving, this gentle reminder to remember the ocean in the frail and small voice of an elderly man. Remembering the ocean, by which he meant remembering the devastation of the ocean that had happened in the last twenty years, they thought again about place, about the responsibilities of writing to place. And thus they continued to circle around and around in this thinking and the sun shone down and their skin sometimes tanned and their skin sometimes burned.

—*Delivered Summer, 2005, Plainfield, Vermont*

THROWING THE BOOK
By Nicola Morris

For me education has been an invitation into a conversation that I previously could only dimly perceive. That conversation happened in newspapers I didn't understand, in people's houses on the other side of whatever town I happened to live in, the side of town where people lived in houses and knew about things. If you grow up with books and ideas and paintings and museums, it is hard to imagine a world without them. But a lot of people live in a world without books and ideas and paintings and museums.

The poet Bruce Weigl writes, "even after I started bringing books home from school, it never occurred to me that they were things I actually had to hold in my hands for very long. It didn't occur to me that I had to read a whole book. I'd never seen anyone read a book in my house, or in the houses of my grandparents. Books were what they gave you at school for homework." His mother saw dangers in books: "Reading some things in books could hurt you." The knowing could be dangerous because there were some questions you were not supposed to ask; things that were better left unknown or unsaid. Weigl grew up believing that "books were useless because they were only words, and words didn't get work done."

As a child I didn't talk much to anyone. When I was sixteen and married, none of my friends read books. It didn't occur to me that I could get a book out of the library. I cooked spaghetti and left the house when someone cooked curry because it made my pregnant stomach heave. I walked the streets and fields and concentrated on being safe.

In high school Bruce Weigl dreamed and made up stories and then enlisted in the army. He was seventeen. It was 1968. In his memoir, *The Circle of Hanh*, he describes a time while he lay ill in base camp in Vietnam when a man from the Red Cross threw a book at him and said, "Read this, boy." Weigl writes, "I kept reading...I don't know why the words made sense to me then...the world must have conspired...so the man could drop that book on my bunk...that book was my link to another world, my bridge to a space blown wide open with a light that filled my brain." He writes, "I was not headed in the direction of books, but there was a moment while I reread and reread *Crime and Punishment* that morning, my stomach raw from bad water, my nerves blown out, my life on a wire, when I must have glimpsed the enormous possibilities of expression because I remember that I was jarred from one way of thinking to another."

The person who threw a book at me was a steelworker in Bristol, England. It was 1970, I had just had a baby and the baby had died. I was living with my husband in a trailer, terrified of having another baby, with nothing to say to my husband. Every night I dreamed I was drowning. I tried to swim to shore but couldn't reach it however hard I pushed my arms in the water or kicked my legs. The dreams infused my days. I worried I was going to die, as, a few weeks earlier, in labor without knowing how babies are born, I'd believed I was dying. The steelworker lived in a bedsitter in a converted Victorian house. His bed was under the window, opposite a fireplace, and he had a hot plate in a corner for boiling water for tea. I was always hungry then, desperate for food and hot drinks. I remember curling in an armchair in front of his fireplace one evening drinking tea, and trying not to eat all of the biscuits in his tin. I told him my dream. I was not a trusting person, but my dream terrorized me. I didn't know anyone who talked about dreams. He didn't try to analyze it, didn't produce words of wisdom. Instead he handed me a book: Carl Jung's autobiography, *Memories, Dreams, Reflections*. From it I learned there was a world within the surface of the world, that everything was not what it seemed, and, most importantly, perhaps, for me at that particular moment, that it was okay to dream you were almost drowning; the danger was if you dreamed you actually drowned. I didn't drown. I also didn't become a Jungian analyst, but I did begin to understand that although I was seventeen, and, within a few weeks, pregnant again, I had wisdom I could draw on.

From that steelworker whose name I've forgotten, I learned I could turn to books, to thinkers, to stories, to dreams, just as Bruce Weigl learned from the Red Cross man that a Russian writing years before could have something to say about the hell he lived in. We both learned to think in new ways.

Eventually I came to America and, with the help of a high school equivalency exam, stumbled into the University of Bridgeport to avoid being deported. I read Richard Wright's *Black Boy*. My teacher wanted to know what I thought. I learned how to live: thinking, writing, dreaming, thinking, some talking, and, finally, writing, writing, writing.

As an MFA graduate you go out into the world that you never left with something to give to the person who asks you for help, even if she doesn't know she is asking. Even if she sits in front of a fire drinking tea, devours biscuits and mentions a dream.

My mother was supposed to be a cook's helper, or a maid. I'm not a bad cook, and I know how to clean a house, though I once got fired because I didn't clean the top of the refrigerator. Still, if I had to I could be a cook's helper, or a maid. But I have the wrong attitude. Books. An education. It has spoiled me, taken me from my station.

You have been spoiled too. Now go out and spoil someone else.

—*Delivered July, 2001, Plainfield, Vermont*

VIII. Literary Activism

ON LITERARY ACTIVISM
By Deborah Brevoort

I'm a political activist. I work on political campaigns, participate in grass roots advocacy efforts, and travel to Alaska every year to work for the Democratic party in the Alaska Legislature.

I'm also a playwright. I've spent the last twenty years of my life writing plays, musicals, screenplays, and now, operas, on a whole variety of subjects.

I dedicate three months each year to working as a political activist; nine months to working as a playwright. My political activism involves a number of things, but I spend most of my time writing speeches, news-letters, and editorials to persuade the Alaskan public about issues that I think are important. I use my playwriting skills when I do political work. They serve me well. What better person is there to write a political speech than a playwright? As a playwright I know how to craft words that fit in the mouth and land in the ear. I know how to hook an audience, grab a spotlight and get a laugh. A political speech is a performance, after all; it is a theatrical event that is delivered by a character, which I also create, and it has the structure of a play. It has a beginning, middle, and end; an inciting incident, a rising action, a climax, and a denouement.

Although I bring playwriting skills to my political activism I do not bring my political activism into my plays. The reason is that I think activism is fundamentally incompatible with art; they go together like oil and water. Although my playwriting skills enhance my political work, my politics have the power to destroy my plays. So I keep them separate.

Activism and art have different aims and purposes. When I sit down to write a political speech, I am setting out to persuade someone of something. My purpose is to convince the listener that we should not dump the tailings from the gold mine into the salmon stream; that Alaskan children deserve health care; that we should prohibit the Alaska Permanent Fund from investing in companies doing business in Darfur. Everything I say has this aim, this purpose—which is to persuade. But the purpose of a play is not to persuade; the purpose of a play is to explore and discover. This discovery takes place for both the writer and the reader, and what is discovered is individual and unique.

When I sit down to write a political speech I know the destination of my words; but when I write a play, I don't discover my destination—and sometimes even my subject—until I get there. Harold Pinter—another political activist and playwright—said this about the process of writing *The Birthday Party*, one of his plays:

"The thing germinated and bred itself. It proceeded according to its own logic. What did I do? I followed the indications, I kept a sharp eye on the clues I found myself dropping. The writing arranged itself...when the thing was well cooked I began to form certain conclusions... But by that time, the play was its own world. It was determined by its own engendering image."

So how does this square with the notion of activism—especially coming from one of our most politically active playwrights? Well, it doesn't. What Pinter is suggesting here is that writing a play is not about expressing an idea or a point of view. It's about exploring something you don't know, as opposed to telling someone something you do.

Someone once asked Flannery O'Connor why she had Hazel Motes, the lead character of *Wise Blood*, kill Solace Layfield by running him down with a car. She responded that she didn't have him do it. He just did it. The person then asked if she planned it. She said no—she didn't know he was going to do it until he did it. She was as surprised as everyone else. She then went on to say that authors couldn't expect to surprise an audience or reader if they didn't first surprise themselves.

What these two authors are getting at is the essential mystery that's at work when you write creatively. I think it's because creative work comes from the imagination, whereas political speeches come from the mind. Even though you use both of these faculties when you write plays and speeches, the imagination and the mind are two very different creatures.

Writers from the beginning of time have talked about the sensation that they are not in control of their work; that when they write, it feels like something is speaking through them; that their work is being given to them from some unknown source, and that they are simply the conduit through which the work is being manifested.

I have this experience all the time. I read my own plays in utter amazement because I don't remember writing them. They seem to know things that I don't know. They are smarter than I am. Wiser. I don't know where they come from. I know where my speeches come from, but not my plays.

I don't mean to suggest that we writers are idiot savants and that we simply channel the work. We don't. We are participants in the creation of it. We are more than participants—we are slaves to it. If you have been given the writer's gift you must make enormous sacrifices to develop and hone that gift so that you can more perfectly manifest the work that comes through you. As Lewis Hyde in *The Gift* says:

> "All artists work to acquire and perfect the tools of their craft, and all art involves evaluation, clarification and revision. But these are secondary tasks...they do not—cannot—begin until the materia, the body of the work is on the page or canvas."

Leaving the purposes of art and activism aside for a moment, I want to talk about a real life situation where art itself became a form of activism.

In 2005, I received a grant from CEC Arts Link to travel to the Czech and Slovak Republics to interview the ringleaders of the Velvet Revolution of 1989, which marked the end of the Soviet dictatorship in Czechoslovakia. I conducted these interviews as part of my research for my play *The Velvet Weapon*, inspired by the revolution.

The ringleaders of the Velvet Revolution were theatre artists. Vaclav Havel, a playwright, orchestrated the revolution from the green room in the Magic Lantern Theatre in Prague with a group of actors, directors, musicians, and stagehands. When it was over he was sworn in as President with artists taking key posts in the government. A puppeteer became a member of parliament, a rock musician the foreign minister, and actors became top advisors.

There were things about activism and art that I learned by interviewing the artists who did this and by studying the works of Vaclav Havel.

The first was that Havel, one of the leading political figures of the last century, was not a political playwright. He was a metaphysical playwright. His plays did not address political subjects; they addressed spiritual matters—the loss of metaphysical certainty, mankind's relationship to eternity, the loss of meaning, and the loss of identity. His plays were also absurdist comedies full of humor, fantasy and playfulness.

Havel's plays were banned and he was thrown in jail for seven years for writing and staging them. When he wasn't in jail, the police would conduct raids of his house in the middle of the night to try to find his manuscripts, which he kept hidden in the trunk of a tree in the backyard.

Although Havel acknowledged that all art has some political impact—whether intended or not by the author—he was opposed to political theatre. He believed that ideological debates in the theatre are "fundamentally inappropriate." He said: "The discovery and truth found in art should not be used to control people."

During this time, when Havel was also the world's most famous political dissident, he would attend writers' conferences and listen to speeches that "the task of literature today should be such and such." He was opposed to this because, he said, literature has no task, except to "keep on doing only what it wants to do. The only hope for literature, he said "is to ignore the tasks that anyone assigns to it, no matter how good their intentions."

Describing his own plays and productions in the theatre, he wrote:

"We didn't try to explain the world; we weren't interested in theses, and we had no intention of instructing anybody. We were playing a game...except that our game somehow, mysteriously, touched the deepest nerves of human existence.

Our humor, which had no connections with the 'burning events' of the time, gave expression—strangely, and indirectly—to the most urgent matter of all—what man really is. The audience felt that even the most grotesque escapades...[on stage] touched something essential in them, something as fundamental as despair, empty hope, bad luck, fate, misfortune, groundless joy."

The communist regime did not prosecute and jail as vigorously those writers and artists who wrote overtly political, anti-regime plays; instead, they jailed those writers like Havel whose work was not political but, rather, "artistically penetrating."[9] What can we conclude from that?

The essence of the conflict in Czechoslovakia was not a confrontation between two ideologies (the communist and the liberal) but a clash between, as Havel says, "soulless, immobile, paralyzing power—and life, humanity, being and mystery."

Havel concluded that theatre and the written word must have a kind of "'heightened radioactivity'—otherwise they wouldn't lock us up for it!" When art is just being art, and when literature is just being literature, Havel says, "It sets our drowsy souls and our lazy hearts moving."

In 2008, Havel came to Columbia University, where I heard him speak about the power of art, plays, theatre, and books. He said that a good play or book has more power than an army. (This from the man who stared down the tanks from the Soviet Union.) He said that the power of art is invisible—that's why the regime considered it so dangerous. They couldn't "see" it and therefore couldn't control it. He also said that just because you can't see the impact of a play or book in a direct way, doesn't mean it's not there. Because it is.

Lewis Hyde, in a terrific book called *The Gift*, compares the radical power of art to gift-giving. All over the world, gift giving rituals work in invisible ways to create community, strengthen bonds between people, and create obligations. In Southeast Alaskan native cultures, for example, anyone who receives a gift is obligated to give a gift to someone else in the community, and to increase its measure. So, if someone gives me twelve blankets, I am now obligated to give someone else fifteen blankets, or something else of greater value. The ritual isn't complete until I do so and under the rules of the ritual I have not fully received the gift of the twelve blankets until I've given the gift of something more.

Lewis Hyde says that this is the way art works. When you write a play, or novel, or poem, the same dynamic is set in motion in the larger community: "A work of art is a gift that has the power to change us by awakening a part of the soul. But we cannot receive the gift of art until we can meet it as an equal." In other words, a work of art awakens something in us and activates us to pass it on in some way. This is why it's so dangerous. It sets in motion a life force that is viral and that can't be controlled.

Hyde also says that most artists are brought to their vocation when their own gifts are awakened by the work of a master. "That is to say, most artists are converted to art by art itself."

I think this is true. Most of us can point to the moment when we were awakened to art; to the moment that set us on the path to writing. Mine was in San Francisco in 1987. I was on a business trip and went to the American Contemporary Theatre one night to see *Angel's Fall* by Lanford Wilson. I was sitting in the Geary Street Theatre. The theatre was half full. The audience hated the play. They were leaving in droves. But I was mesmerized. When the teenage character delivered his monologue in act two about playing tennis, my life was changed.

I don't play tennis. I don't even like tennis, but I walked around for several days in a state of bliss, compelled to meet the power of that monologue—and the play—by rendering something powerful of my own. When I got back home, I started writing. I haven't stopped since.

Lanford Wilson doesn't know he changed my life. *Angel's Fall* was a failure. The critics panned it. No one produces it. It's out of print. But I wouldn't be standing here today if he hadn't written it.

My point is—the power of that play was invisible—but that doesn't make it any less real or any less powerful. As Eric Bentley the theatre critic says... "What happens to you personally when you encounter a work of art may seem like a rather small incident when compared with the invention of the atom bomb, but must you have an inferiority complex about it? The arts depend for their existence on our respect for such 'small' incidents."

To return to the issue of activism.

When we use our art to achieve a political purpose or to promote a point of view, we not only strip it of its power, but we devalue it. By demanding that our plays and stories accomplish some other purpose, be it political, social, or religious, we impose a utilitarian function on them and a requirement that they be useful—the implication being that they're not. What we are saying when we mix activism with art is that art by itself isn't enough; that art has no intrinsic value; that it's somehow wanting; and that it has to earn its keep. When we do this, we buy into our culture's antipathy toward art, and our society's view that it has no value.

This is something the Communists in Czechoslovakia understood all too well. They didn't jail the playwrights who were writing "anti-regime plays." They didn't have to. They were already jailed. They had jailed themselves by putting their artistic spirits behind political bars. Because their work didn't activate and enliven the hearts and souls of the audience, it had no power. It wasn't a threat.

You know the most radical thing that you can do? Write your play. Submit yourself to the "gifted state" of creation and wrestle your work to life. That's how you'll change the world.

—*Delivered Winter, 2009, Plainfield, Vermont*

I KNOW HOW IT ENDS

By Michael Klein

In 1988, the only thing that was happening in my life was A.A. and people with AIDS. I was living with an architect in a loft in Brooklyn that had once been a picture frame factory, still trying to figure out what to write now that I was coming out of the coma that had been my drinking life. I was afraid to say anything out of this new thinking because my only subject in those early days of not drinking was, well, not drinking, and gratitude for living, and I couldn't find the prose for gratitude that hadn't been laced with syrup.

So I read: poetry, mostly, because early sobriety messes with your attention span (you basically have none), and poems were short. I also always sort of knew what poems were talking about, and they usually inspired me to write. Once inside poetry, I wanted to read poems that turned to AIDS because my beauty aesthetic (which hadn't been flattened by booze) knew that one of the tasks of a poem was to make something lyrical out of something horrible. Everything felt like I was reading myself back into being a writer.

But I couldn't find any poems about AIDS. So I wrote one called "Naming the Elements" about a friend who had just been diagnosed HIV-positive. Then, Jean Valentine told me about Mark Doty's title poem from his first book, *Turtle, Swan,* which she had heard him read at Vermont College and so now there were two poems. Then I wrote a letter to a poet asking for another poem, that I actually now might make a book of poems about AIDS, and that poet sent a poem back. And so, I wrote another letter to another poet and eventually a desire for a certainty led to a two-year project of gathering poems which culminated in an anthology called *Poets for Life: 76 Poets Respond to AIDS.*

I knew there had to be a specific response to a new way we were living that could emerge as poetry, but the only thing that qualified me to put together such a book was a hunger to read something that hadn't been written yet. Homesick—as David Kalstone once described Elizabeth Bishop—for a place I had never been. I never thought that making a book like that one was a particularly activist act. Like most activism, the call to action was an innate response to a lapse in the collective consciousness.

At its most organic, I suppose literary activism is the exact opposite of literary success—at least that boring kind of literary success that beginning American writers always seem to be dreaming about: best sellers, huge advances—the screwy consumerism a creative act can get filtered through. None of that kind of attention is particularly destructive, but it is not the real point of writing, which is itself, of course, a kind of activism, but only if it is literary. (I wouldn't call genre fiction, or even a great deal of gay and lesbian writing, particularly activist.)

And while there has been a kind of activism that involves sitting in front of a police horse and writing about it; or talking to a bunch of women about their vaginas and writing about it; or marking 9/11 down as a date of US complicity and writing about it—the kind of literary activism that fascinates me is the one that initiates the resistance to comfortable subject matter, the one about staying true to the art whatever the cost (writing on a matchbook in a prison cell because that's all there is to write on)—the activism located in the psyche of writing itself and not necessarily in writing as manifesto.

There's a terrific story about Mary McCarthy which got curiously imbedded in the description of a writing workshop Andre Dubus III was teaching at the Fine Arts Work Center in Provincetown. McCarthy had just finished a manuscript—a novel—which she had promptly lost somewhere. Because this was in the days before computers McCarthy's original was the only copy. At a party some time after all this happened, someone said to the writer: "Why not just rewrite it—remembering what you can along the way"—or advice to that effect. "Oh, I couldn't do that," Mary McCarthy said, "I know how it ends."

Corroborating with a wisdom of the dark is, in itself, an activism because it identifies a moral exactitude in what others would term an impulse. I know how it ends. What possible reason would she have to write the same thing twice?

Marty Moran is somebody else who started again—by not re-entering a book he had already written in order to turn it into a screenplay. Marty, an actor turned writer, wrote *The Tricky Part*, a memoir about his sexual awakening, which occurred in fragments over time because it began as a seduction by a counselor at a Catholic church camp when he was twelve. The book uses the event to unlock a myriad of longings and became the basis of a one-man show that Marty is still taking on the road.

When asked by Mike Nichols to turn *The Tricky Part* into a screenplay that, ostensibly, Nichols would direct, Marty couldn't do it. He tried to do it—writing the dialogue, setting up the scenes, finding places for the camera to look at—but the material had been entered so completely once as an artist that Marty didn't see the point in going into all of it again. I know how it ends.

If, as Thomas Mann has suggested, "a writer is somebody for whom writing is more difficult than it is for other people," it seems most true of those writers who come to the empty page each time with the intention of saying something they've never said before. Truman Capote, James Agee, Gore Vidal, Brenda Hillman, Michael Ondaatje and Michael Cunningham and others, all have written at least one book that is utterly unlike anything they'd written earlier, and that, it seems to me, exemplifies the occupational difficulty Mann is talking about.

The poet Gail Mazur concluded a recent interview, "When you finish a book you have a really urgent desire to have your next poems be different. To leave behind whatever it is you've been doing. For some people it's an incredible trigger. For me, it's almost been paralyzing. I almost forbid myself to worry about that any more. I would hope that there would be more of the world, more history, more courage, in them."

Literary activists step outside the fact that they have written the work, so they can read what it says.

—*Delivered Summer, 2003, Plainfield, Vermont*

OUTNUMBERING THE DEAD
By John McManus

In a letter to James Madison, dispatched from Paris in 1789 while that city was in the throes of violent revolution, our third President put forth the notion, radical both then and now, that the earth "belongs always to the living generation. They [the living] may manage it then, and what proceeds from it, as they please, during their usufruct." But our laws and mistakes, Thomas Jefferson went on to say, should die with us. And if the dead, disturbing us from the grave with their parochial dreams, should cause the living also to grow necrotic, we are to overthrow them—the dead themselves along with their sour ideas and used-up institutions.

Whence will come this vigor if not violence? If, as our founding father too believed, "The tree of liberty must be refreshed from time to time with the blood of patriots, which is its natural manure," his assertions to my pacifistic ear ring as illiberal as they do radical. Victor Hugo just as famously said no army is stronger than an idea whose time has come. If an idea's time could grow magically out of nowhere, ripening like fruit, art might be fairly called frivolous or effete. I argue that, on the contrary, our burden as wordsmiths is to bring time to the ideas in which we most ardently believe, attempting to convince thousands or just dozens to direct empathy toward those whom the dead have given only blinkered, mean proscription.

My point ought to sound self-evident: to seize the world we ourselves inhabit is as easy as writing one well-told story that millions will read or writing a million stories that a few of us will read. Those souls who hold on dearly to dead thoughts won't read them—it's not in their nature—but their friends will, or their children, or perhaps the constituents who vote them in and out of office. The year I was born, Democratic Senator Dianne Feinstein was a city supervisor in San Francisco, doubting the expediency of a gay rights bill that had been introduced by Harvey Milk. Echoing the position of a fellow supervisor along with whom she often cast her vote—Dan White, who would assassinate Milk the following November—Feinstein said, "The gay community is going to have to face it: the right of an individual to live his lifestyle in a way he or she chooses can become offensive."

Now—to put aside how forcefully I despise the word *lifestyle*—while Feinstein eventually cast an aye vote, she continued to oppose measures that would have broadly granted civil rights. I'm your friend, she insisted again and again, swearing that she personally believed in gays' right to exist; it was just that enough of the dead or dying deemed it untenable. Wait around for your rights, went the line of thinking, chill out, you'll get yours soon enough. But thirty years later, the frontrunner in the Democratic presidential primary was telling a gay journalist what her opponents evinced too in their platforms: be patient; other groups took centuries to win their rights; it's imprudent to tell the dead that our age isn't theirs to inhabit.

Books about gay people still aren't published in half the world, and they haven't been published commonly in the West for long. In 2009, most local administrators manage to keep them out of school libraries, and when I was a child in East Tennessee, the notion that gay people could be the subject matter of a book was unheard of to me. If you were a kid in elementary school, you might make certain jokes and play a game called Smear the Queer, but the idea that real queers were in our periphery seemed fantastical. If I'd encountered one, I might have run off in disbelief. I think I was twelve when I stumbled upon *Dhalgren*, by Samuel Delany. It had been inevitable that I would get around to it, since I'd made it my mission to read every science fiction novel in the Blount County Library. This was a low building with shadowy aisles that has since been abandoned, and I would lurk between shelves reading texts that predicted interstellar travel within my lifetime. Often they made me feel unfortunate to have been born in the benighted past. One day I was standing there reading *Dhalgren*, getting my bearings in a devastated city whose sky shone with two moons and a red, swollen sun, when suddenly two boys, or maybe a boy and a man, were kissing. I read the passage over again, decided it scared me, and returned the book to the shelf, glancing to my left and right to make certain no one had seen me put it there.

Some years later my family was vacationing in a city large enough to have a Barnes & Noble, and in that store I found a novel by Jim Grimsley called *Dream Boy*. It told the story of a boy in the north Georgia mountains who falls in love with the kid who drives the school bus. In retrospect I have to judge it not especially well executed, but after I read it in one sitting (inside the store, lest someone see me purchase it), it did nothing less than make me feel impossible things were possible. In that way, its solution to a problem in my way of thinking was as elegant as special relativity must have seemed to Einstein: at once it rendered simple something that had always been hopelessly and enormously complex.

For books like these to seek us out and tell us our untold stories does nothing less than alter human nature. If Harold Bloom would disagree about my particular examples, he grants that texts possess this power. According to the preeminent critic, without Shakespeare we would think and feel and speak differently than we do. "Our ideas would be different" in a manner as profound as butterfly-effect weather theory might indicate. Hamlet and Falstaff represent "the inauguration of the personality as we have come to recognize it," Bloom said, and without them we would not *overhear* ourselves. Our consciousness would be less conscious. If books that most people have never heard of hadn't changed me irrevocably, I might be inclined to dismiss this most establishmentarian of examples, and with it the more radical idea I attempt to hold up with it. But they did change me, and the funny thing is, I wouldn't list *Dhalgren* or *Dream Boy* among my dozen or even a hundred favorite books, whereas a novel I've named often as my favorite, *Blood Meridian*, was written by a man who scoffs at the notion that we should ever protest any war. In one of his rare interviews, Cormac McCarthy has cited the same philosophy summed up in his great, nihilistic novel: "War was always here. Before man was, war waited for him. The ultimate trade awaiting its ultimate practitioner."

As blindingly original as McCarthy has been, many dead people have argued that all that has always been always will be. There has always been religious conflict in the Middle East; men have always died of incurable plagues. The idea that something should be because it "always was," holds little water with me. Slavery has always existed and in fact there are more chattel slaves now than in any other time in history, but why fight it? It's human nature, McCarthy assures us, and ours is but to observe and chronicle. His view and mine overlap when he insinuates that we writers must grasp human nature better than other people do. But smallpox was always around until it was eradicated, and mainstream indifference to AIDS seemed like it would always be around when Larry Kramer wrote *The Normal Heart*, a play that in a workshop I might call angry and unctuous but that in practice almost single-handedly began the political response to AIDS in America.

Can a text be overtly political and true to itself? I've given but a few idiosyncratic examples from which no conclusion can be gleaned. With enough time I could enumerate countless works whose genius in scoring political points is not just social but literary, yet it has struck me lately that in my own writing I fail to bring straightforwardly political ideas to the same state of full realization as my ostensibly apolitical work. Again and again I have described a certain unpublished novel of mine as an exploration of the failure of artists to spark political change in regard to the Iraq War. In writing that book I kept a quote from Thomas Mann above my desk—"A writer is someone for whom writing is more difficult than it is for others"—because I was having such trouble finding the phantasmagoria I needed to balance out literalness, whereas by contrast it feels easy sometimes, even instinctual, to take up the old template of the sensitive boy in the rural South, whom no one loves or understands, and use him in a story that bears no sleeve on which to wear politics but that will, if I do my job properly, increase the amount of empathy that exists on earth.

But one tires of running in place. If I didn't possess a fool's hope that I can change the world, I might never pick up my pen. The number of ideas I would like to relegate to the dead is too massive to grapple with. One of my best teachers in graduate school wrote an acronym, *KISS*, on manuscript after eviscerated manuscript he handed back to our class. *Keep it simple, Stupid. Keep it simple, Stupid*: over and over and over. Perhaps those whose hearts don't bleed can muster simple stories. Here is the closest I've been able to come lately, in the book I'm now writing, titled *A Mist Went Up From the Face of the Ground*. The first-person narrator, Sebastian, has fled to New York from his life as a West Texan named Bart and his marriage to a woman he believes he's given AIDS. For years Bart/Sebastian has been sneaking away from their home in the High Plains to have sex at bathhouses. Eventually his wife, a Christian Scientist, falls ill with pneumonia. Because of her dogmatic adherence to her religion, Linda refuses to see a doctor; as her condition worsens, Bart grows certain he's exposed her to HIV. In New York, he falls secretly in love with the novel's other protagonist, Hank, a journalist who claims to believe in lying for the sake of advancing a particular cause. For example, he defends the actions of disgraced New Republic reporter Stephen Glass, saying that if Glass's made-up exposé on D.A.R.E. succeeded in turning even one person against that program, then Glass was right to have lied. When Bart discovers that Hank is falsifying his own non-fiction articles, he considers blackmailing Hank into being with him—a development simultaneous with Linda's arrival in the city at a time when Bart is sure he has killed her.

This has turned into the same baroque and labyrinthine plot I somehow always end up with, and I tried to summarize it once by saying it "attempts to examine, through the lens of small-town homophobia, the increasing indifference to AIDS among gay men and how that can lead to deception and atomization." But I don't think it does that anymore, if it ever did. I tried to make it do that, subconsciously anyway, and decided I was writing a bad book. By the time I'd turned it into what I hope is a not-bad book, I found that its moral calculus differed from mine. The villains who inhabit my own politics weren't able to be the book's villains. A section of the text that polemically opposed a religion of which I felt suspicious was becoming a strange, splintered study of faith and doubt. Nor could "bugchasers" anymore be villains. Bugchasers were one of the subjects my character Hank invents an exposé on: men who eroticize the idea of their own seroconversion. Horrifically, these people really do exist, but Hank increases the phenomenon by many orders of magnitude in order to create outrage, a fractured version of which I too hoped to foster. But the villainy of these bugchasers was swallowed by the villainy of my protagonist's lies. I found it impossible to condemn anything while simultaneously trying to increase the amount of empathy that exists on earth. Even Stephen Glass, as obliquely as I was presenting him, fell short as an antagonist. Glass's only mistake, claims my own lying journalist, was in failing to lie more often about important political causes, thus using his lies to change people's minds. I myself, I'm told, should disagree with that claim—and I do, mostly—but there's some perverse part of me that would like to rally behind it. Because writing a novel can take even longer than changing the world, and I hunger for an easy way out. Because it can seem impossible to change minds that are in thrall to the dead, and because the dead, being dead, cannot deal with us in good faith.

Vaslav Nijinsky, the Russian dancer, kept a journal as he succumbed to schizophrenia. In the summer of 1927, he took his wife and daughter to a chalet in the Swiss Alps and, over the course of a few meticulously recorded months, lost his mind. First he shed the ability to discern effect from cause: for instance, he was thirsty because he drank water. He decided the saddest thing to him was that birds were being killed by plane propellers. Woodrow Wilson and the British Prime Minster David Lloyd George were evil for having entered World War I, thereby sending so many deadly planes up to destroy birds. Woodrow Wilson should have been killed before he could cause so many birds to die. Ultimately the solution was simple: he, Vaslav Nijinsky, would build a bridge across the Atlantic Ocean so that armies could drive across it in cars, and the planes would be grounded, and the birds would live.

I'm not well-versed in the history of literary activism. Recently I wasn't sure how to pronounce the word *usufruct*. And I know nothing about oppression when I compare my life to those being lived in Burma, Zimbabwe, Gaza; or when thirty million of us are literally enslaved at this moment, suffering the horror of a practice most of the West believes to be dead; or when 15,000 children die each day of malnutrition. That works out to a child every six seconds, and in my book my character Hank likes to self-righteously point that out, clapping his hands to the beat of the passing seconds—one two three four five *clap*, one two three four five *clap*—whenever he needs to trump a political argument that he's losing. Yet he does nothing himself to help the hungry. And in the end, I'm not sure I can make the claim I would like to make, which is that, for the very reason that I'm writing about this made-up man and the results of his invented actions, the same can't be said of me.

—*Delivered Winter, 2009, Plainfield, Vermont*

AFTERWORD

THE ALCHEMY OF THE WORD
By Paul Selig

I like days like this. I like any occasion where people who care about one another convene. I like the opportunity to celebrate the work of our graduates and to sing the praises of the faculty who work with such love and care to develop the next generation of writers. I like the opportunity to address a community that is conscious, and by that I mean people who are aware of who they are beyond the things that separate them from one another.

When I was in my twenties, most of my friends were dying of AIDS, or at least it seemed that way. And I was absolutely terrified of dying as well. I suspect this fear, as much as anything else, was the reason I began to study energy healing. It was a way to insure my own continued well-being as much as it was a way to care for those friends of mine whose bodies were beginning to unravel and waste away before me. I began to study healing, I think, because it was a gesture that was gentle, and while some friends of mine were marching in the streets, fighting for change, I found myself studying in a seminary, because I had begun to believe that all change occurs first within the individual, and that it is out-pictured, manifested, in form only after it's been given form in the mind.

I suspect that I bring this up to you as a way of explaining that prior to this time, I was a deeply unconscious young man. I valued career over just about everything else, and I suppose that if, in those days, I believed in God at all, I would have believed in a deity that favored one man over another.

I've been through a lot in the last twenty years, and while I do not feel that I have come into consciousness, I do feel that I have woken up a bit, and that this allows me to say the things I am going to say to you now.

Now, I want to talk a bit about unity and separation. I am actually of the belief that we are all connected in a vast and outrageous way, and that part of our task here, in this life, is to remember that, and not in an intellectual way, but in a way that's completely experiential and profound. Our job is to get to that actual place where we can walk down the street and bear witness to the creation that is before us, to the true magnificence that is inherent in each man and woman.

I believe that the struggle of our time is in the remembering of this, in pushing up against the resistance that demands that we remain in the illusion of separation, in the duality of right and wrong, red and blue, black and white and any other way that separation out-pictures itself in our world. I believe it is our duty, finally, to witness the divinity or the humanity or whatever you want to call it in our neighbors, because that is the only way that worlds can heal, and I believe that it is our duty as artists to enter into those places that are kept most secret in ourselves, and bring them to light not so much that we may be healed, but so that others might.

I found myself in an odd conversation several months ago with someone who was asking me how our program was progressive, and how it related to the mission of the college, which is a progressive school with a firm commitment to social justice. And I found myself becoming frustrated by my own lack of agility in the rhetoric of progressivism because I was not able to articulate the obvious, which is that the role of the artist is to reflect humanity in order for humanity to be able to see itself, to feel itself, and consequently to accept itself and thereby change itself.

We are the agents of change. We always have been. We always have been the alchemists who brought forth the Word into manifestation.

What happens here at Goddard is, in my opinion, alchemical. And the reason that people leave this program so profoundly changed is that Goddard requires the whole person to come to her learning, and as the whole person is taught, the whole person is then engaged, and the whole person leaves, transformed, more in command of her craft and more aware, that is to say, more conscious of herself as an artist in the world.

I want our students to have left this place more awake. More awake to themselves as artists, more awake as co-creators of their reality and more awake to the limitlessness that is their consciousness. I want students to be aware that the only separation that exists between them and the person sitting beside them is that which exists at the most superficial level; that in our essence, we are all connected and unique and magnificent in our being. I want our students to understand that the charge they will have as Goddard graduates is to bring their work forward into the world and to demand that it be work that matters to them, and that it calls others to it, so that they, too, may become aware, or conscious, or awake.

Now I want to tell you a little story that I like. It's a true one, and it speaks directly to the role of the artist as a social activist, and, perhaps, to the mission that we all have before us.

A number of years ago, a woman I knew, the literary manager of one of the most important theaters in the country, was having a spiritual crisis. She felt that the work her theater was producing was meaningless and the only people who could afford to attend it weren't the people she wanted to reach. And she was afraid of all the choices she had made, because she believed that theater had become an elitist art form and she had become one of its de facto gatekeepers. And Mother Teresa happened to be coming to town and this literary manager had always harbored a secret wish to be of service.

So she took the train and stood with the crowd outside the U.N. where Mother Teresa was meeting with delegates, and when she came out, my friend shouted to her from behind the barricades, and Mother Teresa stopped, called her out of the crowd, and asked her what she wanted.

And my friend said, "I want to come work with you—I want my life to matter," and Mother Teresa looked at her and asked her what she did for a living here, and my friend, embarrassed, said, "I work in the theater." And Mother Theresa smiled, and said, "In my country, there is a poverty of the body, and that is the work that I do. In your country, there is a poverty of the spirit. Stay in the theater."

I believe that this is a time of great and finite change. And I believe that we have been called, as artists and as teachers, as those in touch with the Greater Creative Mind to call into being the forms and the stories and the lessons that will assist this planet in transforming itself into a conscious world. One that is fully awake.

So I give you praise now, for your work here, and I give you to the faculty who will present you, I am sure, with far more eloquence than I have addressed you with today. If you don't know you are valued here, you are, and if you don't realize how magnificent you are as you stand before us, we are very proud to be your witness.

—*Delivered Summer, 2008, Plainfield, Vermont*

Contributors' Biographies

KYLE BASS is a New York Foundation for the Arts (NYFA) Fellow and a Princess Grace Playwriting Award finalist. His plays have been produced by The Kitchen Theatre, Appleseed Productions, Armory Square Playhouse and the Syracuse Stage *Backstory!* program. A Pushcart Prize nominee, his work has appeared in *Stone Canoe, Folio* and *Callaloo*. Kyle also teaches playwriting at Syracuse University and is Resident Dramaturg at Syracuse Stage. He holds an MFA from Goddard College.

RYAN BOUDINOT is the author of *Misconception* (Grove/Atlantic, 2009), a finalist for the PEN USA literary award, and of *The Littlest Hitler* (Counterpoint, 2006), a *Publishers Weekly* Book of the Year. His work has appeared in *McSweeney's, The Best American Nonrequired Reading, Real Unreal: Best American Fantasy*, and other anthologies and journals. His novel *Blueprints of the Afterlife* is scheduled to be published in 2012 by Grove/Atlantic. He is a Writer in Residence at Richard Hugo House in Seattle.

DEBORAH BREVOORT is an award-winning playwright whose works have been produced and published around the world. Her plays include *The Women of Lockerbie, The Poetry of Pizza, The Blue-Sky Boys, The Velvet Weapon, Into the Fire, Signs of Life* and *Blue Moon Over Memphis*, a Noh Drama about Elvis Presley. Her musical works include *King Island Christmas* and *Goodbye My Island* with composer David Friedman, and *Coyote Goes Salmon Fishing*, with composer Scott Richards.

REBECCA BROWN'S twelfth book, *American Romances*, a collection of gonzo "essays," released by City Lights in June, 2009, won the Publishing Triangle's Judy Grahn award for non-fiction in 2010. Brown's other titles include *The Last Time I Saw You, The End of Youth, The Dogs, The Terrible Girls* (all with City Lights), *Excerpts From A Family Medical Dictionary* (Granta and U of Wisconsin) and *The Gifts of the Body* (HarperCollins). A frequent collaborator, she has written numerous texts for dance; a play, *The Toaster*; and *Woman in Ill Fitting Wig*, a book-length collaboration with painter Nancy Kiefer. Her work has been translated into Japanese, German, Italian, Norwegian and Dutch. She recently co-edited, with Mary Jane Knecht, *Looking Together: Writers on Art* (University of Washington Press), an anthology of writers' responses to work at the Frye Art Museum. She lives in Seattle.

JAN CLAUSEN's books include poetry, novels, a volume of short stories, and the memoir *Apples and Oranges: My Journey through Sexual Identity. If You Like Difficulty* (Harbor Mountain Press) and *From a Glass House* (IKON), both poetry collections, appeared in 2007. The recipient of writing fellowships from the NEA and the New York Foundation for the Arts, Clausen has published her poetry and fiction in many print and web periodicals and in anthologies such as *Poems from the Women's Movement. Boston Review, The Nation,* and *The Women's Review of Books* have featured her book reviews and literary criticism.

KENNY FRIES is the author of *The History of My Shoes and the Evolution of Darwin's Theory,* which received the Outstanding Book Award from the Gustavus Myers Center for the Study of Bigotry and Human Rights, and of *Body, Remember: A Memoir.* He is the editor of *Staring Back: The Disability Experience from the Inside Out.* His books of poems include *Anesthesia* and *Desert Walking.* He has been a Creative Arts Fellow of the Japan/US Friendship Commission and the National Endowment of the Arts, a Fulbright Scholar to Japan, and has received a grant in innovative literature from Creative Capital for his new book *Genkan: Entries into Japan.*

BEATRIX GATES *Nada Que Ocultar/Nothing to Hide,* translated by Yolanda Moreto, will be published by Spain's puerta del mar in 2011. Gates' collections include *Ten Minutes* and *In the Open,* a Lambda finalist. Gates and Electa Arenal translated Jesus Aguado's *The Poems of Vikram Babu* (Host), for which they received a Witter Bynner award. Librettist for "The Singing Bridge," Gates and composer Anna Dembska received NEA support for the opera. Gates' non-fiction appears in *A Woman Like That.*

ELENA GEORGIOU is the author of two poetry collections: *Rhapsody of the Naked Immigrants* (Harbor Mountain Press, 2009) and *mercy mercy me* (University of Wisconsin Press, 2003). She also co-edited (with Michael Lassell) the poetry anthology *The World Within Us* (St. Martin's Press, 2000). She is a is a recipient of a Lambda Literary Award for poetry, an Astraea Emerging Writers Award for poetry, and a New York Foundation of the Arts Poetry Fellowship.

BHANU KAPIL is the author of four collections of poetry/prose: *The Vertical Interrogation of Strangers* (Kelsey Street Press, 2001), *Incubation: a space for monsters* (Leon Works, 2006), *humanimal [a project for future children]* (Kelsey Street Press, 2009), and *Schizophrene* (Nightboat Books, forthcoming 2011).

SUSAN KIM's plays include *The Joy Luck Club* (DPS); *The Arrangement; Where It Came From; Open Spaces; Memento Mori* (Smith & Krauss); *Pandora, Dreamtime for Alice* (Farrar Strauss, DPS); *Rapid Eye Movement; Seventh Word Four Syllables; Death and the Maiden*. Documentaries: *Paving the Way* (WGA award); *Imaginary Witness: Hollywood and the Holocaust; The Meaning of Food*. Books: *Flow: the Cultural Story of Menstruation* (co-written w/Elissa Stein); *City of Spies;* and *Brain Camp* (co-written w/Laurence Klavan).

MICHAEL KLEIN is the author of the memoirs *Track Conditions* and *The End of Being Known* and two books of poems: *1990* (Lambda Book Award, 1993), and the forthcoming *then, we were still living* (GenPop Books, 2010). He has been teaching in the MFA Program at Goddard College for fourteen years and for about the same amount of time, summers at the Fine Arts Work Center in Provincetown. He lives in New York City and Provincetown, Massachusetts. Visit: www.boypoet.com twitter: @boypoet

NEIL LANDAU's film and TV credits include *Don't Tell Mom the Babysitter's Dead, Melrose Place, The Magnificent Seven, Doogie Howser, M.D., The Secret World of Alex Mack, Twice in a Lifetime*, and MTV's *Undressed*, and the forthcoming 3D animated feature, *Tadeo Jones*, from Warner Bros. He is the author of *101 Things I Learned in Film School* (Grand Central Publishing) and a contributor to *WriteNow! Screenwriting* (Tarcher/Penguin). Visit: www.NeilLandau.com

AIMEE LIU (CO-EDITOR) is author of the novels *Flash House, Cloud Mountain,* and *Face* (all Warner Books) and the memoirs *Gaining: The Truth About Life After Eating Disorders* (Grand Central) and *Solitaire* (Harper & Row). Her books have been translated into more than a dozen languages. She also has co-authored more than seven books on health and psychological topics. Liu is a past president of PEN USA and lives in Los Angeles. Visit: www.aimeeliu.net

JEANNE MACKIN is the author of *The Sweet By and By* (St. Martin's Press), based on the life of nineteenth century spiritualist Maggie Fox; *Dreams of Empire* (Kensington Books), a domestic comedy set in Napoleonic Egypt; *The Queen's War* (St. Martin's Press), a novel about Eleanor of Aquitaine and the Courts of Love; and *The Frenchwoman* (St. Martin's Press), a romance set in revolutionary France and the Pennsylvania wilderness. Writing as Anna Maclean, she is author of the Louisa May Alcott mystery trilogy (NAL); the most recent is *Louisa and the Crystal Gazer*. She is also the author of the *Cornell Book of Herbs and Edible Flowers* (Cornell University publications) and co-editor of *The Norton Book of Love* (W.W. Norton). She was the recipient of a creative writing fellowship from the American Antiquarian Society and her journalism has won awards from the Council for the Advancement and Support of Education, in Washington, D.C. She lives with her husband in upstate New York.

DOUGLAS A. MARTIN is author most recently of a novel, *Once You Go Back* (Seven Stories Press). Other works include: *Branwell*, a novel of the Brontë brother; *They Change the Subject*, stories; *In The Time of Assignments*, poetry; and *Your Body Figured*, a lyric narrative. His first novel, *Outline of My Lover*, was named an International Book of the Year in the TLS and adapted by the Forsythe Company for the dance-theater-film piece *Kammer/Kammer*.

ROGELIO MARTINEZ's most recent play, *When Tang Met Laika*, was produced at the Denver Center this year. Martinez is an award winning playwright whose plays have been developed and presented at many theaters across the country, including the Public Theater, Oregon Shakespeare Festival, Mark Taper Forum, South Coast Repertory, Perry Mansfield, Marin Theater Company, Primary Stages, and the Atlantic Theater Co. He is an alumnus of New Dramatists. During his time at New Dramatists, he was the recipient of a Princess Grace Award and the Joe Calloway Award. His one act play, *Union City...*, starred Rosie Perez and was the winner of the James Hammerstein Award. Martinez is a recipient of an NEA/TCG Grant and a Sloan Grant (the latter led to the writing and development of TANG/LAIKA at the Denver Center). Martinez has received commissions from the Atlantic Theater Co., South Coast Repertory, and the Arden Theater Co. He is currently working on a play for the Arden Theater, *Wanamaker's Pursuit*, to premiere in April of 2011. In addition to teaching at Goddard College, Martinez teaches playwriting at Montclair University and Primary Stages.

JOHN MCMANUS is the author of three widely praised books of fiction: the novel *Bitter Milk* and the short story collections *Born on a Train* and *Stop Breakin Down*. In 2000, he became the youngest-ever recipient of the Whiting Writers Award. His fiction has also appeared in *Ploughshares, American Short Fiction, Tin House,* and *The Oxford American*, among other journals. McManus lives in Norfolk, Virginia. In addition to teaching at Goddard College, McManus teaches at the MFA creative writing program at Old Dominion University.

NICOLA MORRIS (CO-EDITOR) is the author of a book of essays, *The Golem as Metaphor in Jewish American Literature.* Her poems, stories, and essays have appeared in anthologies and in print and web-based literary journals. In addition to teaching in Goddard College's MFA in Creative Writing Program, she teaches in the English Department at SUNY Cortland.

VICTORIA NELSON's books include *The Secret Life of Puppets; Wild California: Stories; My Time in Hawaii: A Polynesian Memoir; On Writer's Block; A Bestiary of My Heart: Cautionary Tales;* and *Gothicka,* forthcoming. She lives in Berkeley, California.

RICHARD PANEK's latest book is *The 4 Percent Universe: Dark Matter, Dark Energy, and the Race to Discover the Rest of Reality* (Houghton Mifflin Harcourt, 2011). The recipient of a Guggenheim Fellowship in Science Writing, he has often written on astronomy and cosmology for *The New York Times* as well as *Smithsonian, Discover, Esquire, Outside,* and many other magazines. His previous books include *The Invisible Century* and *Seeing and Believing.*

RACHEL POLLACK is the author of thirty-one books of fiction, nonfiction, and poetry, including the award-winning novels *Unquenchable Fire* and *Godmother Night.* She is one of the world's foremost modern interpreters of symbolism in tarot cards. Her work has appeared on every continent, in fifteen languages. A graduate of New York University and Claremont Graduate College, Rachel has been on the faculty of Goddard's MFA program for nine years.

RAHNA REIKO RIZZUTO is the author of the American Book Award-winning novel, *Why She Left Us,* and *Hiroshima in the Morning,* a memoir about living at the original ground zero during the September 11th terrorist attacks. She is a recipient of the U.S./Japan Creative Artist Fellowship, and the Associate Editor of *The NuyorAsian Anthology: Asian American Writings About New York City.* Her work has appeared in the *Los Angeles Times, Salon Magazine, The Crab Creek Review, The Huffington Post, Mothers Who Think, Because I Said So,* and *Topography of War,* among others.

PAUL SELIG has served as the director of the MFA in Creative Writing of Goddard College since 1998. His work for the stage has been produced internationally and includes plays, operas and text for dance. His channeled book *I Am the Word: A Guide to the Consciousness of Man's Self in a Transitioning Time* was published by Tarcher/Penguin in 2010.

JULIANA SPAHR's latest book is *The Transformation*. Her next book will be called *Well Then There Now*.

JANE WOHL, Ph.D. lives in Sheridan, Wyoming, where she teaches English and Literature at Sheridan Community College. Her book of poetry, *Beasts in Snow*, was published by High Plains Press. She has taught in the Goddard MFA program since 1995.